THINGS MY THERAPIST DOESN'T WANT ME TO SAY

THINGS MY THERAPIST DOESN'T WANT ME TO SAY

Ten Years Post Heart Transplant

Emma Rothman

NEW DEGREE PRESS

COPYRIGHT © 2022 EMMA ROTHMAN

THINGS MY THERAPIST DOESN'T WANT ME TO SAY
Ten Years Post Heart Transplant

ISBN

979-8-88504-552-0 *Paperback*
979-8-88504-878-1 *Kindle Ebook*
979-8-88504-669-5 *Digital Ebook*

For my parents, whose unconditional love
has carried me since the beginning.

For my donor, who lives forever within me.

And for Eunice, thank you for falling
off a chair and saving my life.

CONTENTS

A NOTE FROM EMMA

When I was twelve years old, I woke up surrounded by people in white lab coats, and they all had logos on the left side of their jackets I couldn't recognize. As my eyes adjusted to my surroundings, nothing looked or felt familiar; I had no idea where I was, what bed I was in, or who the people were standing in front of me.

The last thing I remembered was my dad bribing me with ice cream to go to the doctor's office for a blood test. It was the usual "get through the doctor's appointment and then there's an ice cream sandwich waiting for you" kind of tradition we always had. Now, according to these people I didn't know, it was five days later.

What started out as a gimmick turned into a doctor's visit that changed my life.

Nurses and doctors were surrounding my bed which, in hindsight, should have been a massive red flag that I was not okay and definitely not going to get ice cream anytime soon as my dad had promised. Monitors connected to me were screaming a language I couldn't understand, and I was exhausted.

Doctors mentioned the words "heart failure" and "transplant" like they were part of our everyday vernacular, but I could only focus on the number of wires and tubes coming out from under the white hospital bed blankets, never mind the strangers surrounding me. Why was it so difficult to move my body?

I distinctly remember my doctors saying, "You were really so sick." To a twelve-year-old who had never had surgery before or even broken a bone, my context of being "so sick" was contracting the flu or getting the common cold.

Prior to my transplant, I was in and out of school for weeks. I knew my body didn't feel normal, but I had no forethought anything could be this serious. During the day, I was tired and could barely stay awake for half of a school day. I got to know my middle school nurse, Mrs. K., very well because I spent more time in her office than I did in the classroom as I got sicker. My dad would get the call and come pick me up from school in the morning just hours after dropping me off.

Normally, I would've wanted to watch TV with him or sit down for a good meal together, but at the time, all I could muster the energy for was a couple of hours at school each day. After my afternoon nap, I ate dinner and went right back to sleep for another nine hours. My family and I thought I had mononucleosis, or "mono," because many of the symptoms overlap.

There was never any indication it was a heart problem.

Waking up in a new hospital after having a surgery I had never heard of until after the fact is not merely "being so sick." It's a complete conversion. I began to divide my life into two eras to orient myself to my new normal: life before my heart transplant and life after.

Those first few days, weeks, and months post surgery felt like years. I focused on getting out of bed every day and rebuilding my strength because that was what I thought I needed to heal, to get past this. I wanted nothing more than to be back to *normal.* I didn't realize my heart transplant had already forced me to create a new variant that derived from what my other twelve-year-old friends were doing.

My normal revolved around taking timed medications every twelve hours, growing up overnight, and understanding things most normal twelve-year-olds don't. In hindsight, imposing a normal standard—who even really knows what that means—on myself when my body had gone into end-stage cardiac arrest, my heart had failed, and a heart transplant had been necessary to keep me alive seems so silly. I never gave myself the time or space to process how I was feeling until I literally couldn't move from the emotional grief.

Until 2018, seven years later, when I started working with my psychologist, I believed there was only one way to feel about my lifesaving gift and it was grateful.

Over the years, I kept wishing for a hand to come and grab me from this reality I never felt was truly mine. A transplant was supposed to cure me of all this. In a way, writing this book has become the helping hand or even the friend I wish I'd had growing up with a chronic illness. Even ten years later, begrudgingly, it feels as though I am still recovering from being knocked on my ass at twelve years old. Since the moment I woke up from my heart transplant surgery, I have been trying to control my time, thoughts, and feelings to compensate for my lack of control over my health as a kid.

When I first started writing this book, I was very interested in research studies about trauma and the brain and what professionals had to say about recovering from life-altering experiences. Rather than feeling and reliving the stories I was writing, I thought if I could take an objective angle, I could take the easy way out without anyone noticing.

I was wrong, and the writing was shit.

Writing this book has been fucking difficult, and it turns out you can only avoid your feelings for so long. I am grateful to have people surrounding me who guide me toward this conclusion sooner rather than later. My mission in writing this book is no longer to synthesize studies about heart transplants and trauma or write what I think people want to hear.

Paradoxically, the more vulnerably I wrote, the more I realized I am still processing my thoughts and feelings about the last ten years. I deceived myself, thinking I had organized my feelings in nice, neat little filing cabinets deep within my brain. Over ten years later, it has rewarded me the perspective to give myself the grace I didn't know I needed as a twelve-year-old.

This is not the book that is going to give you some bullshit ten-step guide to living life to its fullest. If you want that, pick up any magazine on the shelf after New Year's. I don't have the answers. I am by no means an expert or a doctor, nor do I speak for everyone in the transplant or disability community. Still, if I can promise you one thing, it's that this book is as real and unfiltered as it gets about growing up with medical trauma.

Because living truthfully and telling the truth are risks that I am still grappling with and just beginning to process.*

Although it felt like it at first, my story is not unique. Twenty-eight thousand other individuals received lifesaving transplants—from both deceased and living donors—the year I had my heart transplant (National OPTN Data (All Donors), 2022). Thousands of people grapple with the same intricacies, hardships, and marvels of receiving or giving the extraordinary gift of life.

Since then, that number has almost doubled, even during an ongoing pandemic. In 2020, the United Network for Organ

Sharing (UNOS) reported over 35,000, and in 2021, over 40,000, transplants in the United States, which is nothing short of remarkable. (UNOS, 2021) This shows that organ, tissue, and cornea donation and transplantation are happening all around us all the time.

While it's more comfortable to talk about the data and how many lives transplants have saved, it's just as important to acknowledge there are hundreds of thousands of people waiting for the phone call from their doctor that an organ is viable for transplant.

Currently, there are about 106,000 people, including children, on the national transplant waiting list in the United States alone. Surprisingly, this number is the lowest it has been since 2014, when the list rose above 120,000 people (American Transplant Foundation, 2022). There is no shortcut to conceptualize 106,000 people, and it is even more difficult to accept that people die every day on that list. (Health Resources and Services Administration, 2022)

I say this spiel so often that sometimes I forget the gravity of those numbers and that I was part of the roughly 120,000 people waiting on the donation registry list ten years ago. My life was in the hands of a stranger making a decision, and I am writing this book to honor them the only way I know how—by telling my truth.

This book is something I wish I could have given to my younger self, and my hope is you'll relate to the chronic messiness of life.

I got a second chance at life, and the following stories are my vulnerable truths that honor and celebrate my ten-year heart transplant anniversary.

---

*To share my stories throughout my trauma and recovery journey, I had to ask, listen, and learn from my family and loved ones to help complete or offer perspective on the narratives I wasn't awake for. In an effort to respect the individuals in this book, I have changed names for some level of anonymity. All thoughts and perspectives are mine as I remember them or as I was able to understand from what others shared with me.

MY NEW FRIEND

The last thing I remembered on March 26th, 2012, was one failed blood drawing attempt.

Looking around the room, I didn't recognize any of the faces surrounding me in white lab coats. I assumed it was still the same day my dad had taken me to get my blood drawn in New Jersey on March 26th. I was a kind of sore I had never felt before, and I was so confused. Why could I barely move my torso? It took all of my energy to tilt my head a couple of inches before I realized that I didn't recognize my surroundings.

The smell of the plastic tubing wrapped around my face was so strong I was sure I was eating it, and my words were barely audible when I tried to speak. Instead, a machine that was breathing for me trapped my tongue. In the most twelve-year-old way I could, I thought, *What the fuck happened?*

Eventually, after scanning the room, I recognized two familiar faces: my parents. They seemed oddly calm, considering I was in such a foreign place. My mom didn't come with us to the doctor's office, and now she was in my room in pajamas. The hospital room I was in looked different from the last memory I had getting my blood drawn in my doctor's office.

One of the strangers was speaking to me, and my parents were at my side, but I couldn't focus on what they were saying.

My brain was too clouded from the sedation and pain medications, but I was already trying to piece everything together before I heard my name and "heart transplant" in the same sentence. One thing I was certain about was my dad saying I was sicker than the doctors had originally anticipated. Was this what he meant?

One of the doctors finally included me in the story and shared, "You had a heart transplant."

If I wasn't intubated,* I would've loved to scream so loud the tubing down my throat would burst. Barely moving my arms, I felt a long, narrow, and plasticky taped rectangle in the middle of my chest. With every inhale and exhale, the tape strained my skin. During those first five minutes, these strangers standing around my bed became the people responsible for saving my life.

One of my doctors explained I had had a surgery that I had never heard of before while I was sedated.* *So, my own heart used to be here,* I thought as the plastic tape crinkled the more I tried to test my body's strength and to move. While I was curious to see what it looked like under the plastic, I had absolutely no intention of feeding into my curiosity.

I used to replay the moment I woke up from my surgery in my head over and over again afterward because I was afraid of forgetting. I desperately wanted to ingrain every detail in my head. I convinced myself if I remembered every moment, whether sedated or awake, I could grasp control over my story—over my body.

---

*At the end of the book, there is a glossary with all the medical terms and diagnoses I write about throughout my journey. Words marked with an asterisk (*) are defined or explained in alphabetical order for accessible navigation.

Remembering every moment also meant I could participate in the conversation surrounding my heart care and body. My parents were there to experience every waking moment of the fifteen days I was in the hospital. They had a head start on speaking the language and knowing my treatment team before I did. They were making the decisions that saved my life, and I couldn't actively participate.

If I forgot, I was terrified I would lose even more autonomy, and I wasn't willing to lose another piece of myself that everyone else was there to experience. Every detail mattered to me, but no one felt comfortable talking about it beyond the surface level, and I didn't know how to ask questions.

However, my brain had other plans and a self-preservation agenda. Our bodies are so intelligent that we do not have to click a button or hard reset our brains to tell it some bad shit is happening and we need to shut down.

The brain wants to forget, and some neurologists argue it needs to forget, yet my stubbornness clings onto these traumatic memories, hoping to find answers in them that not even my family knows—and they were there. I want to be able to pick and choose which moments stay and which get overridden so that my transplant doesn't consume my identity.

There are moments before my transplant—twelve years of them—that I never want to forget, but it feels like my life truly started after my transplant.

It's easier to remember the following days in the hospital because most days were the same. I was playing catch-up on all the stories and people I had missed while sedated for six days. Every morning, the sound of a portable X-ray machine clanking through my room door and the sunrise woke me up.

Usually, I could fall back asleep despite the rest of the hospital waking up and coming alive. Before rounds, when all my doctors and nurses met outside my room and then came inside and stood around my bed interrogating me, I had an echocardiogram* and an EKG.*

I didn't know these tests would become a staple in my life or how calming it would be to receive almost immediate feedback that my new friend was healthy and doing well. In those moments, I learned I could trust my body for a few minutes because I wasn't worried about the mini palpitations or chest spasms being another heart attack. The healthy results spoke for themselves.

During the day, things were happening to me and all around me. Every hour, nurses checked my vital signs, and every two hours, an IV alarm would go off, signaling I needed a refill on whatever medication cocktail the doctor prescribed. Surprisingly, the rhythm became comforting, and I started knowing what to expect daily based on the sounds of alarms, shoes in the hallway, and nurses' badges clanking when they entered my room.

By day three, I knew what hypertrophic cardiomyopathy* was and how it destroyed my old heart. Nurses had me sit upright during the day while I learned more about my condition. The muscle tissue around my heart was too thick, causing it to overwork itself.

Sitting in the chair was excruciating. The muscles in my chest felt like they were sliding down my torso. Every time I coughed, sneezed, or moved too abruptly, my chest contracted. Squeezing a pillow against my chest every time I moved was the only relief.

I'll never forget being told by one of the members of my care team, "Not even childbirth is this painful. If you can get through this, you can get through anything." Obviously, to a twelve-year-old, that was super relatable and the motivation I needed to hear to get out of bed. Unsurprisingly, I still felt like shit, constantly needing pain medication to get through the long days of seeing every type of specialist.

I had no idea how I would get the strength to get out of the bed when my nurse said I had to walk around the unit. But I did. That was the first moment on my new journey when I had to blindly trust my body to get me up and out of the bed after it had failed me not even a week before.

I wish I could have left my body and been able to watch myself, to see the strength my parents and loved ones saw. They witnessed every uncomfortable echocardiogram, unsuccessful blood draw and IV attempt, and sick days where I was so exhausted I didn't move.

My first walk out of bed was barely three hundred yards to the corner lounge occupied by family and friends during and after my surgery. I had heard so many stories about people who had come to visit me, and I finally was going to see the room where it all happened.

I knew what I imagined it all to look like in my head, but to actually see it for myself was motivating. My family was so loud nurses kicked them out of the lounge on multiple occasions, and I thought about that every time I was back in the unit. The lounge around the corner from my room had bay-like windows. Sitting there, looking out the windows, my dad pointed out different landmarks, bringing me back to life. The outside world remained the same.

My life no longer felt familiar, but Yankee Stadium was still holding baseball games, and traffic was still blaring below us like any ordinary day.

When I was discharged from the hospital after fifteen days, the same strength that had propelled me out of the hospital bed led me home and into recovery. There were get-well cards, posters, and handmade blankets decorating my bed at home. I felt like a stranger in my safe haven. I didn't feel like the Emma those cards were addressed to. It had to be someone else.

While I was in the hospital, my town had already found out about my transplant and was supporting my family—especially my older sister, Keri, who was still living at home while my parents were with me in the hospital. Throughout my time in the hospital, our communities rallied around my family. Keri operated blood drives, food and gift donations, and card-making sessions at our high school.

While I had been desperate to leave the hospital, now that I was home on my own without nurses, doctors, and monitors to track my vital signs, I remember freaking the fuck out. My parents had a binder and a bag filled with all my medications sent home with them. Just like that. How could my parents and I be responsible for taking care of this precious gift? How could I be trusted to know and listen to my body? I had missed all the warning signs before ending up in the hospital, so how would I be able to trust myself again?

After taking some time to settle in at home, experiencing mundane things all over again was terrifying. After learning how to fall asleep amid screaming monitors and being woken up every hour, the quietness of our home was a stark reminder we were on our own now.

Something as simple as taking a walk with my mom the first week I was home from the hospital required more strength than I thought I would ever get back post surgery. The hill where I learned how to use my bike breaks without training wheels was the same hill that showed me over time I could trust my body with my new heart.

Walking up the hill with my mom, I pieced together the feelings I sometimes experienced before—the dizziness, vibration in my chest, or lightheadedness—were not my fault or from the lack of water I drank that day. My heart had just been exhausted from having to work so hard. After being pent up in the hospital, all I wanted to do was be outside and play in the backyard like I used to do with my sister and dad on the weekends.

All I wanted to do was be a child again instead of transitioning into a new relationship with my body and care routine.

Originally, I anticipated the only new addition to my care routine would be taking antirejection medication* twice a day for the rest of my life. I imagined I would never have to go to the doctor again. I had my transplant, and it made sense that I was better in my twelve-year-old head. Whenever someone else in my life was sick, they received medicine or, in extreme cases, had surgery, and they were better.

Two days later, my parents and I were back in the car on the way to Manhattan for my first outpatient checkup. It's common practice that most transplant centers hold a clinic a couple of days a week for patients to be seen by their medical team pretransplant and posttransplant. It was mid-April, the very beginning of what should have been the last marking period of sixth grade, and instead of sitting in history class with Mr. Rupert or playing scooter hockey in gym class, I was going back to the hospital twice a week.

The blood draws I had on those clinic days were a direct portal to one of the most traumatic days of my life. And I was getting them twice a week, often multiple sticks at once. My arm turned into a pincushion, and I was running out of room on my arms for new Band-Aids and bruises from the needle sticks. All the pokes and sticks were happening to my body, and I just had to sit there and close my eyes.

I didn't have the words to express this then, but I imagine I was feeling the trauma of the day I blacked out and then woke up six days later with a heart transplant. It wasn't until many years later that I finally realized how violated I felt, and still do, when I have to have procedures I don't want. On some days, the violation turns to anger that blood draws have to be part of my care routine—another thing I don't have control over.

My body felt detached from me, not mine, in those moments.

The further out I am from the day I had my transplant, the less frequently I need to go for checkups. That first year was one of the most critical periods to analyze my body's relationship to my new heart,* specifically, how my immune system* reacted to my heart and the antirejection medication those first few years.

I still have my vitals monitored, but now that I am no longer in pediatric care, the responsibility to maintain my health is mine. There are no colorful book illustrations on the walls or TVs playing cartoons when I go to the doctor anymore, and the people filling the waiting rooms are triple my age.

It's an unpleasant reminder that this is my life now at twenty-three years old.

STARTING OVER

Before my transplant, I had never been admitted to a hospital before, never seen an intensive cardiac care unit, or had a blood draw. I wasn't your typical pretransplant patient who would often be in and out of the hospital and dealing with any multitude of preexisting conditions. Hypertrophic cardiomyopathy decided to wreak havoc in my body for a reason no one could explain.

I had a mostly normal childhood, as in I didn't grow up sick or live in the hospital because of congenital heart disease.* It's common for pediatric patients to have multiple heart or lung surgeries before needing a transplant. Still, as far as anyone was aware, I was healthy until the moment my body started going into end-stage cardiac arrest.

I am really hard on myself for getting upset that it took me so long to adapt to this lifestyle, but I have to remember that living with a heart transplant wasn't always part of my life. I still vividly remember certain aspects of my life before my transplant and how simple that was.

Apart from the abrupt onset, starting over isn't always a bad thing, and in a way, my transplant forced me to reset. Starting over can be freeing, a reorientation of your

surroundings with which you may have gotten too comfortable going through the motions.

Except my reorientation was nothing like that. At first, it sucked.

There was no time to pause and become acquainted with my new healthy body. I wanted to stay on track with my classmates and started summer school just a month after my transplant. The business of learning to take my medications on time, doing schoolwork, and restrengthening my body left little time for pausing. I still wasn't completely adjusted to my surroundings when I started high school two years post-transplant. High school is a really hard time to grapple with identity for anyone, let alone someone beginning to process trauma.

It continued to suck throughout high school. My parents had very little, if any, structure to work with. When I was discharged* from the hospital, they received a white binder defining transplant terms and who to call in case of an emergency.

But what about the day-to-day stuff? Like having a sleepover at a friend's house and having to call their parents and have a conversation about the necessity of taking my meds* on time, or what to do if something were to happen while I was there, or asking for individually wrapped snacks and goodies at birthday parties to try to eliminate the chances of sharing germs. My parents didn't have a template to follow when checking in with my middle school nurse to make sure I took my meds on time or how to ask for an update about any illness or virus spreading around school that my immune system couldn't handle. We were even unsure about having visitors in our home because we were so scared to rely on my fragile immune system.

These seemingly normal aspects of our lives before April 1st were no longer status quo. Even six years after my transplant, I just started to barely conceptualize what had happened to me as a kid and what it meant for me as a teenager.

By the time senior year of high school came around, I wasn't only exhausted but fed up with my identity. The reality of being very different from my classmates became harder and harder to ignore.

During my health class, I was performing CPR on a dummy on the floor, surrounded by students who probably had no idea I had a heart transplant or didn't remember. I was sure I would pass out from my realization that this was exactly what the doctors had done to my body. My new, healthy heart began beating so fast as I imagined myself lifeless in the hospital bed in place of the grimy dummy on the floor I was supposed to be attending to.

It was one of the worst aha moments I've ever had, and it was on the floor, by myself, in a smelly classroom.

Before that moment, I never felt empowered to question what had happened on March 26th or the days following. I wasn't conscious for my emergency intubation,* the phone call from my dad explaining they were not sure I was going to make it through the night, or the decision that was made to move forward with heart transplant surgery as a last effort.

I also wasn't aware I was on the donor registration list* or that I was sick enough to be listed nationally and not just in my tri-state area region. Just seventeen hours later, my transplant surgery process began. Before I woke up from what I later learned was a medically induced coma* six days later, there were a million moments that happened that, to this day, I still do not know about. From looking at the photos, I can barely recognize myself beneath all the medical equipment helping me recover from lifesaving surgery, and those photos are now ten years old.

I can't even imagine how it must have felt for my family to witness it.

The first time I heard details about the fifteen days I was in the hospital was almost two years later when a local newspaper interviewed my parents. The journalist asked me a few questions, and my parents told me I could go upstairs because "it would be boring" to listen to the conversation.

While my parents interviewed, I learned that my body was so unstable that a medically induced coma* was necessary to keep me alive. I transferred to a hospital in New York City in a special ambulance that operated as a mini surgical suit because my doctors didn't know right away that my heart was the problem.

Needless to say, that interview was impactful because I learned about myself as if I hadn't been there. Granted, at the time, I was twelve, and many thought I was too young to understand what had happened. But because we seldom talked about it until I was much older, my body never felt like mine after that.

I said words like "cardiac arrest,"* "coding," or "end-stage heart failure" often, but there was no meaning or weight behind them. While my family unfortunately learned this new language without much choice, I never caught up when they weaned me off sedation medication or during follow-up checkups. My story felt and still feels like it belongs to everyone else but me because we only talked about it in certain settings, and most of those settings were not at home.

My body's health came up a lot in the hospital, and usually only in the hospital: How I looked, how I felt, how the medication affected me. The more we talked about things I couldn't control but just had to medically comply with, the more I felt like a medical dummy. Every blood draw and biopsy* felt like things happening to my body, not me, because I had little agency in these moments.

My team needed something from my body—biological indicators that my heart worked—and they didn't have time to discuss much else. It was and still is frustrating because it's a huge part of my life. I am just my medical record number on a schedule.

In the beginning, I struggled to keep up with my doctors and parents' conversations with such little knowledge about heart transplant surgery during check-up visits. I didn't need to know the name of every valve or the function of each vessel, but a general understanding of the cardiac system and how transplant affects the rest of your body, and continues to as you get older, would have been beneficial.

I wasn't too young to understand what had happened to me, and withholding information from pediatric patients about their own bodies can really fuck with their sense of self and autonomy. Part of starting over was also losing my innocence to gain my independence. I experienced this during my freshman year of college in 2018 when I took a class that examined behavioral and social factors that influence the health of young adults. For the final, we had to do a project on ourselves.

Throughout the year, we were supposed to document our progress toward a personal SMART (specific, measurable, achievable, relevant, and time-bound) goal, and naturally, I picked the most personal project I could: managing my blood pressure. I was supposed to document my blood pressure every day and document the SMART changes I adapted into my schedule to manage my pressures.

Uncoincidentally, my nephrologist* wanted me to do the same thing, so I thought double accountability would keep me in line. Framing my acute kidney failure as the subject for a class final made it less personal. I hoped getting an A in the class would motivate me to take care of myself more, rather than the crippling anxiety of needing another organ transplant.

Nevertheless, I saved most of the report for the last week of the semester, and again I found myself frantically Googling my own diagnoses to write the term paper because I didn't know enough about them from previous conversations with my team.

Instead of talking to my team throughout the semester and advocating for my concerns about my health or asking the questions I needed to answer for the report, I found myself on a WebMD rabbit hole at two in the morning watching cardiac surgeries. The surgeries had nothing to do with the final. I needed a brief synopsis of the connection between blood pressure and heart health. My lack of understanding about my heart transplant subconsciously led me to watch videos that triggered an anxiety attack.

The next morning, when I woke up after a few hours of sleep, I saw a text from my dad that read: "I don't know if you got to sleep or stayed awake to finish the paper, but you know there are those mind-blowing moments when those things don't matter, and you hold something or understand some truth for the first time that is more important than any paper or assignment. I think it says a lot about who you are. I don't think many who had even a heart catheter* would do it. You have a strength and love of life that is extraordinary."

I saved that text because my dad's support along the way has helped me get comfortable with the idea that maybe I am a little too hard on myself at times. Maybe I can be extraordinary and still not know 100 percent of the details or a day-by-day recount of what happened in the hospital.

Ten years have given me the time to pause and remember that as painful as these memories were to experience, they have shaped who I am, and no amount of ignoring them, even for ten years, is going to change that.

Writing this chapter, this book, is the first time in the past ten years I have outwardly asked my family to contribute to my narrative by asking them to share parts of theirs. Avoiding my narrative has not brought me the peace of mind I expected, and this opportunity to rewrite certain parts of it has muddled my intentions for writing this book. I thought this would bring me closure and the answers I needed to clean up this mess, but it has only clarified certain truths.

One of the biggest truths is that I shouldn't have learned about cardiac arrest in my high school anatomy class or senior CPR and first-aid health class when I had gone into cardiac arrest five years prior to that.

But I did. And that is okay.

FINDING NORTH

For as long as I can remember, I get lost too easily. In fact, I still am lost most of the time.

It's one of my many flaws. I can't read a map or follow directions very well. I can nod my head enthusiastically when given directions, but somewhere up in the confines of my neurological switchboard, the wire for processing cardinal directions fried at some point. I can usually get by with landmarks, although that has been a more recent discovery.

Using landmarks to orient yourself is a lot harder when you're in situations you've never experienced before. There is no signal, indicator, or compass to direct you on what to do or what comes next, especially if you're disoriented at such a young age.

As a result, I learned during fifth grade I really like someone telling me what to do. This was how I avoided making decisions for most of the next eighteen years because if I was left to orient myself on my own, there were too many directions to get stuck, lost, or make a mistake with.

School provided a consistent structure that I learned to depend on for guidance. This is quite fucking ironic, considering how much I crave control but am willing to give it away to others. When you're a chronic anxious overthinker, it's a full-time job reasoning with a mindset that yearns for control and consistency.

During my fifth-grade year, my teacher Ms. Long led us through an activity I still haven't forgotten. She handed us a worksheet, and the only instruction given to our class was to read the paper fully; we would get in trouble if we talked to each other.

Naturally, I started reading the instructions at the top of the paper like all my past teachers had programmed me to do. The first direction listed was to read everything before doing any of the activities. I went through each task without much question, following each of the ridiculous questions. If the worksheet my teacher gave me told me to do some jumping jacks, who was I to question it? I was just trying to follow directions.

Most of the other students in my class were speeding through the worksheet. Every class I was in had those kids, the ones that could finish an activity by the time I had barely finished writing my name down on the paper. I always wanted to partner with them, as it seemed like they found north a lot easier than I did.

Then there were the students who were just sitting there. They had done some writing and then continued to watch the rest of the class waste time doing each activity line by line. After about five minutes, our teacher reminded us to read the directions entirely. As time went on, fewer students were standing up doing the activities or writing things down on the worksheet.

Looking around the classroom, it seemed like everyone else could find and follow directions quite easily without needing the context of the full map, whereas I was stuck in the middle of nowhere with no escape plan. When I finally flipped the worksheet to the back side, at the top of the paper, in bold, read, "Now that you have read all the instructions carefully, you don't need to complete any of the tasks. Do only sentences one and two, sit quietly, and watch the other students do silly activities."

After about ten minutes of watching us make fools out of ourselves, Ms. Long ended the activity and asked the class what it taught us. As a fifth grader, I would imagine most of the answers were along the lines of "Following directions is important." What I didn't realize at the time was activities like this one, along with the general public school mold, teach us that if we don't follow directions and instead stray away from what we should be doing, we'll look like a schmuck jumping around while everyone else is sitting there watching.

Or, in worst-case scenarios, we'll be reprimanded for not sticking to the rigid mold designed not to flex or support all types of students, including myself.

So, subconsciously or not, I started to depend on the structure of being told what to do.

When I got to seventh grade, after spending the summer finishing the remainder of sixth grade at my kitchen table, I felt so alone. I wasn't the same person I was the day I left sixth grade and didn't come back. After my heart transplant, when I got back to school, I was essentially an adult.

My kitchen table became the center of my universe. Not only was it a mini classroom over the summer and a small hospital triage room* in between meals but also one of the few spaces where I felt like myself without worrying if anyone understood me. At the kitchen table, I practiced setting up my meds for the week and learned how to get in the habit of coming back to the table every twelve hours to take my meds on time. Most importantly, sitting surrounded by my dad, mom, and Keri, I was trying to grasp how my understanding and bearings of north could change in an instant—overnight.

From what I remember, no worksheet or term paper addressed how to make lemonade when life gives you a shit ton of lemons. Where were the directions for moving forward when I needed them most? Especially after my transplant, one of the most disorienting moments of my life, my parents weren't given a manual on navigating parenting or taking care of a transplant recipient.

Ten years later, I can't truthfully say I have stopped looking for directions. I sometimes fantasize about having a plan to stick to with no more surprises or need for rerouting. Directions are hard because you have to be nimble and change often, but going down a new road is scary. How do you know where north is in new territory? Change is scary.

I am working really hard on finding my north.

The transition from being a student to a regular human is a universal experience that is fucking hard. Instructions ranging from what to wear, when to show up, and where to go are ripped out from under you without much time to prepare. You're left writing your own five-step guide on how to overcome a job interview or decide what is next, figuratively and literally.

While these regulations were restrictive and, most of the time, annoying, I didn't realize how they applied to my life outside of school and homework assignments. All of a sudden, after graduating college, I didn't have a required curriculum that dictated my weekly schedule or a document that out-lined what the next five months would look like, including due dates and time off.

Although true north doesn't change, many moments throughout each day threaten to pivot me from going where I thought I was supposed to.

My dad shared his short rib recipe with me a couple of months ago. It was the first time I had attempted to cook one of his infamous meals without being able to ask him questions in person. I complained to him that I didn't want to mess it up and that it was his fault for setting such high expectations in the kitchen.

I was no longer hovering over his shoulder, picking at whatever he was stirring on the stove. I was over five hundred miles away from our kitchen table when he beautifully reminded me, "Now you are again on a new adventure in a new city, but true north does not change. Keep looking for true north. It is not an end point that you figure out one time and you're done. You will always continue to see where you are."

My dad texted me that message at noon on a Thursday. His reminder has since been guiding me north. In this next chapter of my life, ten years post heart transplant, I am dedicating myself to moving forward and finding that sense of direction within my body.

This notion of finding north is not unique to me or even my dad. North has led generations of people forward, which can be difficult when it feels like the human experience is never on your side. The Big Dipper is one of my favorite constellations because my dad pointed it out to Keri and me so many times that it seems obvious to locate. Yet, it's still surrounded by so much chaos; over a million stars, and still, on most nights, no matter what, that ladle is still prominent and able to be found.

My dad always stresses the importance of finding true north—knowing where you have been before, where you are, and where you want to go.

I had never really experienced true chaos until I was eleven years old and woke up in a foreign bed with monitors and IVs hooked up to my body. When I finally found the strength from somewhere inside of me to get out of my bed to look out the window, the stars that I could see from my deck at home were the same as the ones I saw from the window in every hospital room and the ninth-floor lounge around the corner from the room that became my second home.

So much had changed in such a short period of time that I was desperate to find anything still to ground myself and stick to. Every day in the pediatric intensive care unit was just as overwhelming as the last, if not more.

However, the stars were still the same among all the chaos going on in my life below them. For my anxious brain, all the beeping monitors, new faces, diagnoses, and other medical terminologies I was learning were enough change at once to make me feel like I was living in outer space.

At eleven years old, I had left my body and was looking down at it. I couldn't recognize where I was or even who I was connected to all these plastic tubs and machines pumping lifesaving medication into my frail body. Reflecting on this ten years later, I still am paralyzed by my least favorite emotion: uncertainty.

Some days, it's easier to come back to my kitchen table, wherever it may be, and accept that my body is my home and trust that together, we are moving north. But most days, I'm stuck in the gray area, trying not to let the uncertainty of the future lead me down the wrong path.

After all, where are the directions for how to survive your twenties ten years posttransplant?

TOO MANY HEARTS FOR EMMA

When my mom got the call that I was coding,* she left her office in Manhattan and never went back to work.

No one expected a failed blood draw would land me in the pediatric cardiac intensive care unit (PICU),* let alone for fifteen days in a medically induced coma. My parents had the clothes that were on them and what was in their pockets when they arrived at the hospital.

While in the hospital, it was no longer a secret my heart was failing and I was waiting on the donor registry list* because my whole community knew.

I grew up in a suburb of New Jersey in the kind of town where if something happens, everyone knows about it. My parents had been living there for sixteen years when I had my transplant, and by now, I think my dad knows everyone on a first-name basis, or they know him. People began talking, asking questions, and reaching out, and rightfully so. I had disappeared from our small-town community and had been sick for almost three weeks before my doctors decided to list me on the registry.

Even within my middle school class of about one hundred and fifty kids, rumors buzzed around the hallways about who would catch the heart disease next, as if they were going to catch hypertrophic cardiomyopathy from a sneeze. With my parents' consent, my classmates were all gathered into our school gymnasium to discuss heart disease and transplantation. Despite what everyone had heard, my gym teachers and principal clarified heart disease was not something that spread from person to person like a common cold.

And just like that, my family's community rallied around us in every way imaginable. No one hesitated to bring my parents a change of clothes, hygiene products, phone chargers, home-cooked meals, my favorite blankets, and other miscellaneous things that made the stay at the hospital bearable.

My older sister Keri was sixteen at the time and should've been going to swim team practice every day after school or driving around with her friends who had just passed their driver's test. Instead, she was the messenger between our hospital bubble and the outside world.

Once Keri's school day ended, she helped orchestrate blood drives, bake sales, and card-making sessions. Keri held three blood drives in my honor while I was in the hospital; donors were turned down because there weren't enough time or resources to accommodate everyone. She represented our family while my parents were at my bedside in the hospital. All the cards and posters I came home to were made at the blood drives and bake sales held in my honor.

Yet I had no idea any of this was going on until a few days after I woke up from my surgery.

One of the inpatient nurse practitioners who had spent a lot of time with my family and me reassured me that *I* was in control of who I told. "Your transplant doesn't have to make up your whole identity unless you want it to," she explained. "Many of our patients go on to live normal lives and travel, go away to school, and even move out from their parents' home, which are all things kids without transplants do."

Immediately, I decided I wouldn't tell anyone other than my family. When I shared that decision with my family, it was brought to my attention that people were already wearing purple T-shirts with interlocking turquoise hearts with my name on them.

The purple T-shirts had already decided for me.

The interlocking hearts that originated from a doodle on a hospital napkin turned into Hearts for Emma—a symbol displaying what I was going through on everyone's shirt. My parents also held off from giving me my cell phone for a couple of days, and reflecting on this decision, I understand why. At least fifty messages wished me well and asked if they could do anything for me. People I hadn't talked to in years were reaching out about my heart transplant when I barely understood what one was. My community had found out I had a heart transplant before I did, and my phone was another indicator of something I had lost control over.

As a result, I have always felt exposed. They knew how sick I was before I did. They knew the moment my shit was about to get rocked before I did, and for a long time, I resented that. Twelve-year-old me didn't know it at the time, but the target of my resentment was not at our community for supporting us. It was just an easier emotion to feel and process than trying to make sense of losing so much control.

I couldn't understand how it was my decision to decide who to tell when there was an assembly at my school about me and my medical condition. The discomfort around other people knowing what I was experiencing was not something I was willing or ready to sit with.

So I didn't talk about it unless I had to.

I had thought we were all on the same page about my feelings toward outsiders' involvement in my medical journey, but about a year after my transplant, my parents surprised me with a proposal to start a nonprofit.

My parents called me into their room on a Saturday morning in April. As I sat on the bench at the foot of their bed, my mom started talking about *tikkun olam* ("repairing the world" in Hebrew). "Daddy and I were raised with the value *tikkun olam*, and we feel we need to do our part in repairing our community. Emmy, we've been thinking of turning Hearts for Emma into a nonprofit."

I blurted out, "Why?"

My mom continued, "Remember the blood drives the town ran while you were in the hospital? You probably don't realize it, but 'the power of Emma' was truly extraordinary. Your story brought all these people together to raise money and awareness about organ and blood donation."

I had nothing to say.

"We feel obligated to use that momentum and find a way to give it back to the hospital that saved your life."

My dad chimed in, "The community gave us a lot of money, and we don't feel comfortable keeping it. We think this is the right thing to do."

Defensively, I responded, "Do we have to make it a nonprofit? Couldn't we just donate the money and not make a big deal out of it?"

I was not too self-absorbed to disagree with my parents. I knew there was a need. In such a chaotic time, I am sure it was a relief to rely on our community, from sports teams and family friends to our temple congregation and family from all over the country, leading us north when we couldn't ourselves.

They were all our guiding lights, delivering full-course meals to the hospital lounges for staff and visitors to share, cooking me pasta and risotto because I couldn't stomach the gross hospital food, driving Keri back and forth from the hospital and constantly sending my parents messages checking in on me. But sitting there on my parents' bed, I only thought about myself and how their idea for a nonprofit made me feel.

In 2013, a couple of months after our initial conversation, my parents founded Hearts for Emma as a 501(c)(3), and we had eight board of directors members. I was legally too young to be a voting member of the nonprofit but attended the meetings for moral and experiential support.

Ten years later, I've had the opportunity to reflect on the decision my parents made to establish a nonprofit, the impact it had, and how it made me feel—both then and even now.

I've accepted there was no way to know then what we do now. Writing this story has given me the opportunity and space to reflect on the feelings I had as a twelve-year-old and how they've evolved as I have gotten older and more time has passed since my transplant. At the time, I wish I'd had the skills to facilitate a conversation around how a transplant affects everyone in the family, not just the patient. I felt this, but since my transplant was over, I thought there would be less momentum in the pendulum effect.

In a way, the establishment of Hearts for Emma was an extension of a traumatic and stressful time in my life that I had to continually talk about. My name was on the front cover of it all, and there should've been open dialogue around the effect it was going to have on all four of us. As a kid, there was no way to know that even when things are done with good intentions, it doesn't override the need for consent or the possibility that it can impact people in unintended ways over time.

The interlocking hearts became the emblem of my recovery journey and the glue that brought the nonprofit together.

My feet were dangling off the dining room chair at the first board meeting. I was so young. Based on my parents and my experiences, the original Hearts for Emma board of directors sat around the table and designed Hearts for Emma's mission to support families directly where most organizations can't: bedside.

I am sure survivor's guilt and not wanting to disappoint anyone—even though I didn't want to be the "Emma" in Hearts for Emma—kept me engaged. I didn't ask for my transplant to begin with, and in the spotlight, it was even harder to separate myself from that identity. Despite not wanting to draw more attention to my heart transplant, I knew that I never wanted another kid to be in the same situation that I was in—not knowing what a heart transplant was until after the fact.

What kind of person doesn't want to help other people? I thought, so I went along with it.

During board meetings, I hoped that remembering my experience would somehow make it more real, more mine. When family brought us things from home, like blankets that were soft and smelled like home instead of sterile linen, or the shampoo I liked that got the knots out of my hair instead of the generic hospital brand that resembled water in a bottle, not soap, it made a huge difference.

It matters much more than I realized at the time or could begin to process.

As we spent more time in the hospital for check-ups and procedures, my parents and I observed an obvious need for bedside support. My mom had a blue notebook, her Bible, as she called it, where she wrote down almost verbatim every medication dose and change, every diagnosis, and everything that was said during morning rounds and check-ups. That notebook was her reference point so she could advocate for me when I wasn't up to it or had a question for my doctor that she couldn't answer. My main concern was managing my pain, which should be the case for every pediatric patient.

Yet many kids experience that on their own. At twelve months or nine years old, kids experience the reality of healthcare expenses and other financial stressors because their loved ones can't afford to take off from work to sit bedside with them for an unknown extended period. Or some patients might have a single caregiver in their family who has to stay at home with their siblings while they receive care in the hospital.

I can't imagine going through what I went through without my parents, like when my body was so weak I couldn't even go to the bathroom or get changed without my parents' help.

Overwhelming doesn't even begin to adequately describe what being treated in an intensive care unit is like, and it was upsetting to learn about how common it is for patients not to have loved ones' bedside support. Spending any time in the hospital is scary, especially when you're that sick and there are so many unknown variables—so much so that the language on the PICU is very present focused; "future" means later that afternoon or tomorrow morning rather than weeks or months ahead.

Every day, I met new people who knew so much about me because they had spent the days prior to my transplant getting to know and comforting my parents while they attempted to wrap their heads around their new environment and language—a completely new reality that had transgressed overnight. Imagining kids and teens trying to understand and explain what is happening to their body when my parents barely could is unbearable.

While my parents tended to my needs, Keri and her close friends drew posters and colored pictures to decorate my and other patients' rooms. Posters and photos of our family and friends covered the walls of my hospital room and made it feel less aseptic and more familiar. Being surrounded by love and familiar faces, like a poster of Lalibela, our family's Portuguese Water Dog, was comforting during the nights when I was in so much pain I couldn't sleep or when I was feeling lonely.

It seems superficial that cards or posters of your favorite TV character can make such a difference, but they do. For some families, their loved one in the PICU is states away and they can't visit because of the distance. It's all too common for kids to stay in the PICU for weeks, months even, while they wait for a donor or receive critical care. This is why it's so important to have that bedside support because sometimes there are some real shitty days or even weeks.

That interlocking heart logo has evolved a lot over the last nine years, and the impact it has had on families, patients, hospital staff, and my own family is hard to quantify. Recently, it has come to light how vital medical workers are due to the COVID-19 pandemic. Fortunately, I have witnessed their lifesaving work for over ten years now.

The medical workers that are interviewed on TV or volunteered on COVID-19 units aren't simply just medical heroes. They are a part of my extended family. Nurses and doctors went above and beyond too many times to count, even digging through dirty linens to find my blanket, to make time spent at the hospital a breath easier.

One of the first procedures I had once the hospitals opened back up in 2020, was a routine cardiac biopsy.* I remember one of my favorite nurses who used to run the catheterization laboratory* (cath lab) calling me the next morning to check up on me. She knew that I had had a rough time with my anesthesia and personally took it upon herself to call me to make sure I was recovering okay.

The first patient comes into the cath lab—where patients are admitted and tended to before their biopsy procedure—around 6:00 a.m., and it's nonstop until the last case leaves, which can range from 4:00 to 9:00 p.m. There have been many times I have left that late and arrived when the cath lab opened. It touched me that she took the time to personally call me in between the chaos of her morning.

At the end of our conversation, she mentioned that she was retiring and wanted to individually tell me how much she enjoyed treating me and spending time with my family. That nurse didn't have to call me or wish my family and me well, and the fact that she did is why Hearts for Emma is so special. It's phone calls like that that remind me why Hearts for Emma is so much bigger than my discomfort with attention and, at times, my identity. Although truthfully, at the start, I didn't want to identify as the Emma in Hearts for Emma and still don't on some days.

It was really hard to see the bigger picture of who we were helping when I was still so hurt and traumatized from my own transplant, and it took me years to admit that.

Regardless of the origin of Hearts for Emma, it's just as powerful today as it was in 2013, if not more. Our reach has almost tripled, and not only that, but it also gives me the opportunity to use my voice in ways that wouldn't have been possible without the organization. I understand this now and actively create space for both my gratitude and my discomfort. When I was younger and all throughout high school, I didn't.

I used to do a lot of speaking engagements for organ donation and blood bank advocacy, but the more I performed this role, the more I hated myself for not feeling the way I presented myself: a grateful recipient living life to its fullest. I knew how shitty I felt, and without realizing it at the time, I used Hearts for Emma as a platform to replace my anger about needing a transplant with what I thought I was supposed to feel all the time: grateful.

It has taken a lot of internal work to learn how to say no. Before then, I took it upon myself to continuously advocate for organ and tissue donation and do every speaking engagement for every temple, school, blood drive, and group.

I reasoned I owed it to my donor and never declined an opportunity, no matter how I felt about it. However, it never occurred to me that there are other ways to honor my donor without manipulating my boundaries. I'm working on being more mindful about where I choose to spend my energy and the motive behind it. Is it my survivor's guilt, or am I genuinely interested?

In hindsight, I wish my parents were looking for my consent or blessing when establishing Hearts for Emma because Hearts for Emma continued to feel like an invasion of my privacy beyond my discharge from the hospital posttransplant.

I fought those feelings for so long until I realized it never was about the organization, just my relationship to the cause and how it started.

My parents were just doing the best they could with what they knew at the time and what they felt was a deeply values-based decision. They received little to no resources from the hospital on how to process and adjust as a family to our new normal that was a very sudden transition for them too. There was no manual for them on finding and continuing moving north again.

No one can blame them for that, not even me. Would I have liked for there to have been more of a discussion around the implications of starting this nonprofit and what it would mean for our family? Yes, and I can move toward surrendering to the loss of control at the same time.

I am no longer trying to please anyone else when talking about my experience.

Advocating and sharing my story with others, whether it's to spread Hearts for Emma's mission or when I decide I want to share that part of me with someone, is including the whole truth, even the ugly and uncomfortable parts. Most importantly, advocating for organ and tissue donation is living a life that I *want* to live.

My truths about what happened ten years ago are just as important to the Hearts for Emma mission now as they were then. Part of changing my narrative is owning it and being authentic even when it sucks, even when I would literally rather be anyone other than myself. Especially when my survivor's guilt is laughing in my face and makes saying *no* harder, I can do it.

I admit I am still not comfortable with people knowing my shit, especially medical stuff because it's my silly attempt at controlling my story. I don't want people to know I am dealing with a chronic issue "blah blah" or had a procedure last week.

I want them to see me as Emma: the Emma before my town blew up with blue and purple T-shirts and the Emma now who is coming to terms with her identity as so much more than just a heart transplant recipient.

FOUND AT SEA

I was able to mentally hold myself together until my senior year of high school.

My guidance counselor and I had gotten to know each other quite well, but she was trying to push a boulder uphill in getting me to talk about post-high school plans. I remember crying in the hallway and found myself sitting in her office shortly thereafter. There wasn't anything specific that set me off, but the more I tried to stop, the harder I cried.

I was desperate to avoid another drastic change when I was working so hard to ignore the biggest of them all: the scar running down my chest.

College seemed so far away that it felt pointless to plan for. While I desperately needed to leave my small town and wanted to, I was terrified about not being healthy enough to go to college.

There was barely enough time to prepare for being my own caregiver, and the thought of moving out of my hometown seemed catastrophic. How the fuck would I be able to live alone at college? How would I trust my body to tell me when something was wrong without my parents' oversight? What if something happened when I was alone in my dorm room? I didn't want to answer these questions, so I ignored the college process for as long as possible.

My perspective at seventeen looked quite grim as I sat in an office so tiny it could've been a closet, hyperventilating from crying so hard. She sighed and said, "I feel like I could give you a million dollars, and you still wouldn't be happy." That attempt at comforting me was clearly not a trauma-informed response. I don't blame her, though. My anxiety about what was next debilitated me from looking forward to anything; all I felt was numb.

When it came time to apply for college, I had a really hard time writing personal statements and scholarship essays. Every essay sounded the same in my head. "I am so grateful to be alive and am excited to channel that energy into succeeding at…" At five years posttransplant, I was nowhere near grateful. Most days, I was depressed about my transplant and then angry I was still depressed. While I did receive a heart transplant, there were other super cool things about me that I wanted to talk about but didn't know how to do so in a way that wouldn't make me feel guilty.

At the same time, I wanted to break the tether and finally go somewhere where no one knew me. My hometown felt suffocating. It seemed like everyone knew my secret, and the choice to communicate about it was taken away from me. I no longer wanted to identify as the "transplant girl." I don't really know if that is how people saw me, but that was what I thought.

I wanted to leave that part of me at home and stop talking about it altogether, let alone write about it for blogs, admissions essays, job applications, and so forth. I was a counterfeit optimist, copying and pasting the same things I had read and heard other transplant recipients saying, thinking I should say them too.

When I wasn't trying to convince myself that I was just a normal, average teenager, the rest of my time I was busy persuading myself I was part of this "#GratefulToBeAlive" and "carpe that mother-fucking-diem" crew who are all somehow so good at time management. I wanted to join that clique so badly, and still do sometimes, but the more I forced myself to write about the glorifying aspects of living with a transplant, the more I pitied and hated myself.

I was still grappling with this life change no one prepared me for, and I was expecting myself to fall in love with my experience. A little part of me hoped, under all the walls and tough facade, that the more I wrote about it in this light, it would become abundantly clear why all this had happened.

That was a load of crap.

Managing depression on your own as a kid is really fucking hard. I used to base my understanding of depression on the commercials I saw on TV. All I needed was a pill to make the clusterfuck in my head go away. Regardless, if only I perfected more homework assignments or tried harder in volleyball, my dark cloud would go away because I was living life to its fullest.

The overload of choice paralyzed me, and I drowned from the weight of it all. I didn't realize it at the time, but perfecting the next move didn't lead me to college right away, but instead to the middle of the Coral Sea.

My parents always told me I could swim before I could walk, and I reverted back to that toddler who used to always fall into bodies of water accidentally at eighteen years old.

In my defense, the water was calling my name. My family just didn't hear it.

There is an actual principle, commonly referred to as Archimedes Principle, which explains that in the water, everything that ruminates in your brain or makes you feel the weight of the world on your shoulders still weighs less than water itself. Come to think of it, that is probably how my admiration and love for the ocean started; in the water, nothing is holding you down.

When I am floating, I no longer feel like it's my civic duty to solve the world's problems, or on a micro level, my family's. In the water, I can be present and engage all of my five senses without feeling guilty for focusing on where I'm at rather than where I think I should be.

All of my shit stays on land, even my identity that I felt pulling me under as I swam through the waves. It makes sense that even as a toddler, I was attuned to the frequency of others' feelings without knowing it. About two decades later, I came to learn that is what being an over-anxious empath is.

Most of my fondest memories take place in the water. It's my family's happy place. For most occasions, the Rothman family would find a way to get to the beach. Parents' wedding anniversary? Beach. Birthdays? Beach. Last day of summer before school started? Beach. Mother's Day one-month post-transplant? We piled into the car with three spare outfits for any season just in case I accidentally fell in and found ourselves at the beach.

My dad used to carry me into the ocean and sometimes put me on his shoulders while we jumped the waves. Despite the risks and unpredictable tides, I always felt safe. I knew he would never let anything happen to me.

The year I received my transplant wasn't just significant for me; it was also the year the final season of the *Oprah Winfrey Show* aired on television, and one of the giveaways to the audience was a round-trip vacation to Australia. I grew up watching *Oprah* with our babysitter, and I was mesmerized by this particular episode.

The trip was curated and planned by her team. Audience members experienced picnics on white sand beaches, stayed at five-star resorts, saw the magnificent Uluru sandstone rock, and learned from the Aboriginal peoples. Most of the episode centered around the ocean and exploration of the Great Barrier Reef.

It should come as no surprise, then, that when I had the privilege of fulfilling my Make-A-Wish when I was eighteen, I designed a trip to Cairns, Australia: the Mecca of reefs around the world.

One of the days the four of us were there, we took a catamaran out to the reef. I am not sure if this is common knowledge, but the Great Barrier Reef is not close to the shoreline. In my head, you could walk into the ocean and swim out a little and there would be vibrant colors and exotic fish at my feet. In reality, my family was on this boat, braving massive waves and severe seasickness.

At its closest point to the shore, the reef is nine miles into the water, and at its furthest, ninety miles from shore. We were snorkeling somewhere in between. By the time we got out to the reef, I think my dad and Keri were ready to swim home, they felt so sick.

Since the four of us went in the winter, we had to suit up. Two wetsuits and a three-minute crash course on ocean safety later, I leaped off the boat steps and was weightless. I floated in my safe haven, my happy place, and among my people—the fish. The silence was welcoming.

This was the first time I had ever been so far offshore and in such deep water, and I still can't articulate that feeling. As I had my first out-of-body experience for the day, naturally, our water instructor led us over to a floaty with a red scuba dive flag sticking out of the water to point out "Nemo" to our group.

That was my cue to separate from the group and swim off on my own for a little. As I floated over the coral "bommies," my senses were completely overwhelmed, but not in the way that I was used to or had experienced before. It was overwhelmingly beautiful such that I wasn't fixated on the pounding in my chest. I was comfortable being overstimulated with my medical conditions or even schoolwork. Usually, my body let me know I was feeling the burden before I knew it.

The internal chaos of juggling my identities between being a normal teenager at school, a sick kid at home and in the hospital, an adult at Hearts for Emma board meetings, an athlete trying to overcome my own incurable illness, a good girlfriend, sister, daughter, and friend were no match for what I observed below me.

It was one of the first times in my life when I had the opportunity to embrace all parts of who I was. I thrived being in a new country with my family where no one knew who I was. In other words, it was my first major attempt to stop feeling sorry for myself and start trying to live. My love and respect for the ocean led me to one of the most profound moments of my life.

Little rainbow parrotfish and butterfly fish scurried below me, swimming so fast I wasn't sure I even saw them. As I observed from above, I couldn't imagine having to fend off the ocean every day for survival or a small bite to eat. The best part of observing the marine life was that I could leave that chaos at any time.

The more time I spent in the water, the more I realized the scar running down my chest didn't matter. The pills that keep me alive didn't matter. How I thought of myself didn't matter.

When it was time to get back on the boat, our crew started to make a commotion. My mom and Keri had already taken off their suits and were on the top deck of the boat. Word buzzed around that another large vessel had joined us, but one without an engine. I briefly heard the word "whale" and dragged my dad back into the water without a second thought. I knew Keri and my mom were lost causes.

One by one, they directed us to keep both hands on an old barge. I knew there was a whale in the water. I wasn't sure where, what size, or even what kind. I won't lie or bullshit myself here; I was terrified. We were no longer looking down on the shallow reefs. Not only could I not see the bottom of the ocean, but I couldn't see anything approaching in front of me. The water was so blue and went on for so long that it felt like a mindfuck. There was no way a whale could sneak up on us. How could a school bus-sized animal approach us without noticing?

My dad's body froze, and I remember clinging to him so hard that I felt both of our hearts pounding. Looking right at us was a twenty-five-foot dwarf minke whale. A school bus had snuck up on us from the ocean's depths and was so close I swear we made eye contact. Remembering how the water glistened from its eye and the white accordion-like folds of the blubber under its mouth gives me chills. Just as fast as the whale checked us out, it was gone.

And at that moment, I realized that to the whale, I was just another strangely shaped fish in the sea.

It was one of those instances when my soul left my body and connected to something more powerful than the vessel that holds all of my organs. When I think about it for too long, I get skeptical if it even happened. What I do know is that while experiencing that moment with my dad, holding onto him for dear life, the dwarf minke whale pulled me forward.

And it never would have happened without Make-A-Wish.

WHAT IS A CHRONIC DISEASE? WHO DECIDES?

It has been ten years, and I still don't feel like I am sick enough for the label *chronic disease.*

During the fifteen days I spent at the hospital, no one ever mentioned the phrase "chronic disease." My heart failed, so I got a new one, and I was better. Failure is black and white. Failure isn't chronic; something works or does not. I thought my heart problems were gone, that I was cured after the transplant. My cardiology team could file my chart, which was too thick for my liking, and I would never have to see it again. My time as a patient was over, and I needed to get back to school and my friends.

I was so sure I wasn't like the other kids living in the PICU because my doctors kept reassuring me that my other organs were working perfectly. So once I got back to middle school, I worked hard to ensure that I was doing everything just like everyone else. I didn't want to slow down and take my time. I wanted to be normal and live up to my arbitrary metric for normal. However, this meant being sick often and absent from school a lot, because going at the pace of everyone else was hard, even without a suppressed immune system* or chronic pain.

The special treatment I got during middle school, like having my desk cleaned before every class period or receiving new school materials instead of used ones, was belittling and, I felt, not necessary for the health of my newly suppressed immune system. I didn't want a 504 school plan,* to leave class every day at 9:00 a.m. to take medications, or to have to worry about swine flu spreading around my middle school. All of that seemed extra, like there were strings attached to me on purpose, holding me back from ignoring a huge part of who I really am when no one is looking.

I was so afraid of someone overhearing me and explaining to my teacher that I needed extra time on an assignment because I was in the hospital over the weekend, and even worse, I was afraid to admit to myself that I needed these accommodations. Needing the accommodations meant submitting to the fact my transplant did make me different, and that was a fight I was not willing to give in to. Back then, I couldn't define chronic disease because I didn't want to recognize that normal and chronic disease don't add up to a realistic expectation. In some respects, I still can't.

When I saw myself, I didn't see someone who was sick or recovering from major surgery. I saw the same old me from before.

Later in my life, right before my ten-year anniversary, I took a class called Disability and Pop Culture. One of the assigned class readings was the memoir *The Pretty One*, written by Keah Brown, which helped me understand my experience in ways that brought me so much clarity and relief.

The way Brown articulates her relationship with her cerebral palsy is the same way I have been trying to relate to my heart transplant. She writes, "I fantasize about being able-bodied more than I should. These fantasies are ableist, and they come close to undoing the real work I do every day to remain feeling genuinely cute... In these fantasies, I forget what I already know is true: it is possible to soar in a disabled body." (156)

Reading those words on one of the days I felt so tired and defeated brought tears to my eyes. I had never felt so validated and seen before, and that validation was an exhale I had been holding for the last ten years.

I thought someone with a chronic disease is supposed to look like they have one based on my own internal ableism.* Without knowing it, I had deeply internalized society's perception of people with disabilities or people who aren't the "norm." Before taking the class, from the movies and shows I watched, I had assumed chronic disease had a certain look and stigma attached to it. I thought since no one could see my disability, I didn't have one, and therefore didn't have to deal with that stigma.

Showing people the evidence of living with a chronic illness made it real, and I wasn't ready to accept that. Really, I just wasn't ready to challenge my own internalized ideals about how I felt about my disability, let alone the way media and pop culture define and characterize them.

So I played it off or ignored the questions people asked altogether. I wanted nothing to do with my heart transplant. I thought the whole "medically fragile" thing was in the past once I had my surgery. I didn't want anyone to know why I missed first period or why I often had extended time on most of my assignments. Yet, I had to put all of my time and energy into taking care of myself to prove to myself that I deserved this gift, that I deserved to live.

As you can imagine, that created quite a bit of internal tension. I wanted to control my identity but also completely ignore one major part of its existence.

I continue to grapple with the idea of perceiving my disability as a weakness, as something to hide so people don't see the full spectrum of what having a heart transplant looks like or any discomfort I have between me and my body. When I looked in the mirror, I didn't want to see or feel the disability stigma I ruminated about. Because to acknowledge my disability, I had to accept that I couldn't control receiving my heart transplant.

As much as I detest it, I tie my idea of acceptance to worthiness—accepting that my heart failed me means proving my worthiness of the lifesaving gift I received. I had no idea how to embrace my transplant as part of what makes me *me* and also understand that it wasn't my whole identity. I am working toward letting go of the idea that identifying or labeling myself as chronically ill doesn't make me weak or less of a person, regardless of if anyone can see my illness. It's a lot easier to worry about how others are going to perceive you than it is to worry about how you perceive yourself; one feels out of your control, while the other reflects your self-worth.

I chained my self-worth to my transplant. I thought it was the only thing that made me interesting, yet it was one of the few things I detested talking about.

When I am alone in my bed or writing in my journal and acknowledge that those two words are in fact, a part of me, a quietness hums across my brain. The tension accepting myself is a little less fraught because I am no longer internally fighting who I am. While these moments are few and far between, it's easier to give myself grace when I am alone and can lower my expectation bar. The word "chronic" doesn't have a bitter taste in my mouth. The connotation of "chronic" isn't positive or negative. It's just there. I don't feel judged or imperfect for needing help and demanding less of my body than most.

My bed has always been my place to reset. There are no beeping monitors, people to please, or unrealistic expectations to meet. I can be myself without worrying if I am acting or being perceived as too sick or not sick enough. I don't have to pretend I am feeling grateful or living life to its fullest when I am stuck in bed watching Netflix from a head cold that has taken me weeks to get over. There is no need to mask my exhaustion or bruises from the three tries it took to draw ten vials of blood.

Reframing my own internalized ableism as "undoing the work" I am putting into myself gives me so much clarity. The inverse of reframing fixates my anxious thoughts on my worthiness (or lack thereof)—it continues to manifest my own internalized ableist message that because of my medical trauma, I am not enough. Similar to Brown, focusing on this reasoning counteracts my internal work to let the weight of those thoughts go.

There are a few pages from Brown's book I have earmarked and reread when I need to. They are comforting, especially when I retreat and feel like I don't have anyone to talk to about these things. What surprised me the most was that Brown isn't a transplant recipient, and yet she voiced vulnerabilities that I was feeling and didn't have the wherewithal to say. Fifteen days in the hospital isn't enough time to ask questions or begin to process the *after* of heart failure. The after, I guess, is where the chronic part of the disease starts to seep in. My heart is no longer sick, but that doesn't mean I am done with blood draws, biopsies, echocardiograms,* electrocardiography tests (EKGs),* and countless doctor's visits.

All these aspects of my life are chronic, and for the longest time, I felt like I didn't qualify or have the right to feel that way because my scars are not visible. Brown taught me about

invisible disabilities and how my own perception of myself
was ableist. I didn't have all the language I needed or the
introspective skills to understand my relationship with my
heart, chronic disease, and all of us combined as one person
until ten years later.

Even now, I still hate talking about how I feel in front of
doctors. I am tired of answering the same questions over and
over again: "On a scale of one to ten, how bad is your pain?"
"How are you feeling?" "What medications are you on?" "Have
you been recording your blood pressure?"

It's draining being in the hospital; whether it's for a forty-minute checkup or a three-hour biopsy, it's all the same.
Especially the months following transplant, while spending
so much time in those spaces, I felt like my heart transplant
was all I was, had, and was going to have. There is no avoiding who I am in that space. I am Emma the heart transplant
recipient, and I can't hide or turn that off like I can in school
or in my bed. All of my medical history, both concerns and
successes, are on display and talked about so casually, like
talking about the weather.

"We are concerned about this level because it is elevated
and could mean rejection,"* or "We want to double-check the
fluid around your heart to make sure it has not increased,"
or "We need to monitor this because of the long-term effects
on your other organs." There is so much instability in these
moments because one moment you are mentioning something
minute, like a headache, and then before you can process
what is happening, there are three follow-up appointments
scheduled with different specialists.

Transplant is supposed to provide you with the medical
stability to keep living your life, but for me, it has established
a profound lack of trust with my body.

In the early years, before I understood the fragility of my health, I never expected rejection. The bad heart was gone, and all of that shit was in the past. My parents sent out my results to our family the minute they got the call, and I probably rolled my eyes at their excitement for my good test results. I wasn't staring at my inbox waiting for the results. But then I came across a Facebook post that read, "Remember, transplant is not a cure but rather a second chance at more life..."

It had never crossed my mind that one day my heart could fail again, that I would need more life. Whatever more was, it had to be perfect because I wasn't as cured as I thought. My anxiety played on every palpitation, headache, fever, sore throat, twitch, and every symptom in between because one of them could be a sign I was overlooking that my body wasn't performing well.

What if that heart palpitation was a heart attack and not my anxiety expressing itself as chest pain? What if someone found me on the floor and I couldn't advocate for myself? What if I didn't mention how I was feeling a month ago and then woke up in the hospital again because I overlooked my symptoms and downplayed how I was feeling? I sure as fuck didn't want that to happen again, so the obvious solution was to talk about every little thing. How could I trust my body again?

Shortly after I came across that post, I started seeing a nephrologist who diagnosed me with acute kidney failure. My mind immediately went to the worst-case scenario, and I was sure another transplant was in my future. My parents and I hadn't even left the doctor's office yet before I googled "kidney transplant recovery time." More than my anxiety around my other remaining organs failing, I was pissed. Hadn't I already dealt with the whole transplant thing?

No one told me how stressful transplants are on your body, and stressful is a kind word. Transplants can increase your chances of so many other illnesses because of your body's lack of immune response. That apprehension alone should be classified as a chronic disease: always feeling like you are waiting for the next diagnosis.

My nephrologist must have assured me no less than ten times I wasn't sick enough for a kidney transplant and that most of my treatment would be through medication management, but there were still so many sleepless nights following that doctor's visit. When I woke up in the morning, I was terrified that I would be in a sterile hospital bed with a new kidney instead of my safe and cozy one at home.

My nephrologist isn't the only specialist I see outside of my cardiac team. I regularly see about six other physicians because of the greater risk I have because of a suppressed immune system. When I was in college and taking a full course load, coordinating care was a full-time job on top of the other three I had.

Meeting new doctors and incorporating them into your routine is like dating but worse because you must trust these people to make the right decisions and guesses to keep you healthy. When I was home for Christmas or a few days for Thanksgiving break, my to-do list included seeing my neurologist,* nephrologist, gastroenterologist,* gynecologist,* dermatologist,* and my psychologist, Dr. J. if I made the drive after recovering from the mental gymnastics of seeing so many doctors in such a concentrated time.

Granted, everyone should be on top of managing their health care. I acknowledge what a privilege it is to have access to this caliber of care and the support from my parents' insurance to cover most of the costs of going to the doctor so frequently. We all deserve this kind of care no matter our body's abilities. Especially when you have a chronic illness, putting off that appointment shouldn't be an option because of a lack of access to health care.

There have been many sleepless nights in anticipation of the next morning, not wanting to fall asleep because that would mean that morning's procedure was that much closer, but I have never missed an appointment before, despite my crippling anxiety. I have left lectures, meetings, and exams to take a phone call from a doctor's office because waiting on hold for that call back could put me days behind in scheduling an appointment or refilling a prescription.

I admit that I still need constant verification that my heart is working because I am so afraid of finding myself in another situation of not knowing what happened to me until after. They say as you get older, the chances of rejection slim. However, I still get routine blood work done as if my transplant happened only three years ago, not ten. Seeing the physical results of the blood work is always a breath of relief. In that moment of time, my body does the talking and lets me know everything is working as it should be. I love and crave the reassurance I am taking good care of myself despite all the shit I give myself for not getting seven hours of sleep or exercising every day.

It took a long time to process the blood draw. That was my last memory pretransplant, and the feeling would return every time I had my blood drawn after. Now, it's comforting to know that the discomfort will lead to something I am always craving: reassurance that my body is working well when the lab results come in. The lab results relieve me from wondering when the universe will force me to adjust again, even if it's just for a couple of weeks.

Another disability author, teacher, and activist, Dr. Rebekah Taussig, wrote in her book Sitting Pretty, *The View from My Ordinary Resilient Disabled Body*, "I thought I'd already done all the adjusting the universe would ever ask of me" when talking about losing feeling in her legs overnight without as much as an explanation or clinical diagnosis. (113) Dr. Taussig also expresses a concern that I think about daily: "No matter what I try to do to prevent it or wish it away, any part of my body might stop working at any instant." She follows this with an important asterisk, explaining that this inconvenient truth is true for all of us, not just those of us with disabilities.

The further out I get from transplant, the more and more I relate to this. The detection of kidney failure was a huge adjustment, and that was just the beginning of the universe's accommodation requirements posttransplant. It's familiar to fall into a comforting headspace of waiting for the next bad medical thing. The mindset really doesn't serve me, but sometimes, for a couple of minutes or days even, it's nice to give in to my fear of my body giving out on me again.

In those moments, I hate my body. I am frustrated and annoyed I have to deal with this anxiety and give constant attention to my body. Giving in to the fear offers me permission to feel imperfect and acknowledge that this shit is hard. There is less of an expectation to overcome these feelings because it's just the way it is.

I have a chronic illness.

I HATE THE WORD SHOULD

"We have learned that trauma is not just an event that took place sometime in the past; it is also the imprint left by that experience on mind, brain, and body."
—BESSEL VAN DER KOLK

"Should" is a crap word, and anything that follows it is usually an internal judgment, most often of ourselves.

"I *should* exercise thirty minutes every day, but…"

"I *should* get over the job rejection, but…"

"I *should* ignore the way my family reacted, but…"

The "shoulds" impacted my time at college because I convinced myself of too many "shoulds." Instead of framing my thoughts as *you can go to the gym today*, I talked to myself out of spite that compared what I was doing to what I thought I *should* be doing.

"Should" is part of the imprint left by trauma because we're not doing what we think we're supposed to, whereas "could" is opportunistic. I let the word "should" heavily impact my relationship to change.

My relationship to change has a lot to do with many changes in my life happening at the mercy of my health.

Change terrifies me—so much so that I drag my feet in the mud for as long and hard as I can because I think I should be fighting against the gravitational pull of moving forward. Moving always gives me anxiety because my body has learned to associate change with medical failures. Even at twenty-two years old, I still feel the same separation anxiety leaving my family as I did the first time I moved away from home.

For most of the changes in my childhood, I had no control. Seven years post new heart, I should've had more mental flexibility in letting go of the whole control bit. No matter how badly I wanted, I couldn't go back in time and change what happened. I would dwell on my aversion to change because I knew it should've been surrendered long ago.

Sophomore year of college, I moved into my dorm just like every other kid in their second year of college. It was ninety degrees outside, and my dorm had no air conditioning. As my parents and I were hauling most of my life's belongings to the fourth floor of Dellplain Hall, I couldn't stop the frantic, decision-remorse thoughts spinning around in my head.

That summer, my parents had just supported me through my second lifesaving operation that had nothing to do with complications from my heart. As I watched my mom unpack my clothes and my dad set up the fridge in my dorm room, I started internally panicking. Instinctively, I tried to think of other things for them to help with to prolong move in, even though by then, we were all hot and cranky. When they left, I would be on my own again, and that dependence on myself was bittersweet.

My mind drifted. I was no longer at Syracuse University but back in the emergency room in the city. It felt like it was just a couple of days ago that I was lying in the triage room hooked up to my familiar monitors, hearing the hypnotic beep of the blood pressure cuff suffocating my arm. The pounding on the sides of my temples was starting to dissipate, and I was thankful for the pain management. The medications were strong. I had been throwing up for almost twelve hours before arriving at the emergency room. I hazily remembered my dad arguing with the emergency staff late into the night, advocating for brain scans.

The physician assistants and nurses in the emergency room continued to assure my dad that neurological scans were not "protocol" for migraine pain and that I was ready to discharge and go home once I finished my IV medication.

Piece of advice: never argue with a lawyer. Especially not my dad. From personal experience, you won't win. He is fiercely protective of the people he loves, and his unwavering love for me led me down the hallway for my first CAT scan.* There is nothing my dad wouldn't do for me, and thinking back to that night, I can confidently say we were not leaving the emergency room without a scan. He just knew.

By the time doctors approved and ordered the scan, very few staff were working that late at night, but the brain scan results came all too quickly. A physician assistant wasn't confident with the finding as she came into our little triage room, holding a printout of a WebMD page, to tell us the results of my first brain scan of the night.

She handed my parents the printed piece of paper and said, "We think your daughter may have this, but we'll need to order another scan to get better imaging." She left the room like she had not just delivered a bombshell.

Two hours later, that same physician assistant came back and was, unfortunately, more confident when she referenced the printout she had given us a couple of hours before. However, she wasn't a neurologist and couldn't officially diagnose me with moyamoya disease (MMD).* In layman's terms, I had a blockage in one of the two arteries responsible for supplying blood to the front of my head.

When I looked over at my parents sitting in the chairs next to my bed, my dad's face turned green. I was lucky the pain medication had already been administered and was flowing through my body because it was the only thing that could've softened the blow. Until then, I had never heard of MMD and thought we could address it at home. My IV drip had finished, and I was under the impression I was going home, but I didn't get to go home for three days. Instead, they transferred me from the emergency room and admitted me to the hospital for more tests to confirm the findings from the brain scans.

I came to understand MMD was something serious because every medical person I saw continued apologizing. Many of them saying shit like, "I am so sorry you have to deal with another medical thing," "I have never heard of MMD," or my personal favorite, "You had a heart transplant. After that, you should be able to get through anything. Nothing could be as painful as that."

The hero that is my dad broke the news to me after they had done more tests confirming the diagnosis. He was on his regular coffee run and returned to my room with a look on his face I had never seen before.

I asked him, "I'm going to need surgery, aren't I?"

When my dad burst into sobs, my brain immediately jumped to worst-case scenarios, thinking, *Shit, I am going to die. This is it. My heart transplant didn't do it, but this definitely will.* My dad, who I have seen cry maybe five times in my whole life, was crying with me. He wanted to be the one to break the news to me so I would be prepared for when the doctors came in to tell us I needed surgery.

The same man who got in the car at 4:00 a.m. to meet me in the emergency room four hours away from home, who runs a 5k every year in jeans and boots without any training, who consistently offers to drive halfway across the country to pick me up and take me back home to New Jersey, who has never outwardly complained about anything his whole life, was still able to support me unconditionally, even when he was scared shitless.

He was willing to take on that burden so that later I would be composed enough to understand what would happen to my body.

I had déjà vu that morning, as my cardiac doctors, and now the new addition to my care team, a neurologist, surrounded my bed during rounds and delivered the official diagnosis. I had MMD and needed two surgeries on the right and left sides of my head to help my brain bypass the blocked artery to receive more blood flow and oxygen. I had thought comparing my heart transplant to childbirth was a far reach before, but now I had people comparing getting my skull operated on to my heart.

Reluctantly, I scheduled the first surgery for the second week of July and the second two weeks after.

After the first MMD corrective surgery, the recovery was an uphill battle. When I met my surgeon for the first time, he corrected me, saying, "Technically speaking, it is not brain surgery. I am just operating on the outside of your skull and barely touching your brain." I should've known by then not to listen to the surgeon's timeline for healing, as I was still having headaches that felt like golf balls were shooting inside my head when I was supposed to be healed, according to their clinical perceptive timeline.

When I was consistently in that much pain, it seemed less painful to live with the increasing possibility of having a brain bleed or ministroke caused by MMDthan to go back to the operating room fully knowing what the after was going to look like.

The scars had no time to heal, or even scab for that matter, before I went back to school the first week in August, and they continued to pound as my parents finished breaking down the move-in bags. How could I care for myself without them after all we had gone through over the summer? For the previous two months, I had depended on my parents for most of my needs, and suddenly, I was on my own.

I desperately wanted to pause time. Why was I in Syracuse? Why was school still so important to me if my body was barely able to piece itself together in time for the first day of classes?

My head was still swimming with all the ways I planned to try to avoid answering the seemingly innocent icebreaker question every professor would ask, "What did you do over the summer?" How could I avoid the inevitable conversation of explaining what MMD was when I had yet to really understand myself what had happened? The diagnosis and both surgeries happened within two months of each other, and I should've known after recovering from cardiac surgery that brain surgery would be similar in recovery time.

Instead of trusting myself, I listened to everyone else. It couldn't be that bad. After all, I had already had a heart transplant, right?

Different scenarios played through my head, and all of them sounded attention-seeking. I should've felt comfortable confiding in my friends. They chose to support me and stay in my life and love me for all that I am. But I was so uncomfortable sitting with the two hospitalization memories. They made me feel weak, and I didn't want to be the sick friend or the friend who is in so much pain she can't move from her bed and won't be going to parties. That would mean accepting that both diseases were part of me all the time.

Finding ways to casually say, "My dad saved my life this summer! I had two surgeries to cure an accidental finding of a brain disease that, if left untreated, could lead to brain bleeds, strokes, and a shit ton of other scary, life-threatening, morbid outcomes! Two weeks later, here I am! Back at school. What about you? How was that consulting gig?" was ridiculous. I didn't want to tell anyone, but as soon as anyone asked how I was doing, like a waterfall, I couldn't stop myself from over-sharing how my summer went.

Immediately after doing so, I felt like shit. There wasn't any value behind why I shared what MMD is or how traumatic both hospitalizations were that summer. In fact, I had barely told anyone at home, yet there I was, blabbering to people at school who were probably too drunk to remember our conversation. The desperation to be heard and validated by everyone but myself catapulted the words out of my mouth before I could pause and think about why I shared such intimate details.

It was a trauma competition in my head. My shit sucked more than theirs, and that was all I needed to confirm I was allowed to feel bitter and self-indulgent.

My friends or classmates would share minor inconveniences with me—normal stuff you vent to people who care about you—and without realizing it then, I tuned them out; nothing could be as horrible as neurosurgery. Therefore, I didn't care. The date who ghosted them or the professor who unfairly assigned homework over break was nothing in comparison to the inconveniences I went through—my chronic pain. I knew life was short, and their dumb bullshit drama was a waste of my precious time. No one understood the way I do how precious life is.

My ego was convincing, and I believed no one could understand what I was going through. The fact of the matter is I made those assumptions about the people in my life without remotely trying to let them in and share a glimpse of my mental state.

I had yet to understand everyone has their own shit and making it a competition only made me feel more isolated and distant from the people I really care about. The funny thing is, after my second encounter with a serious, potentially life-threatening diagnosis, I tried to continue with life as usual. Before my MMD diagnosis, I convinced myself I was not chronically ill, I didn't need time to heal, and my body could handle whatever I threw at it without consequences.

My transplant wasn't enough to convince me otherwise, and like most decisions I made before MMD, my health was in the back of my mind. I repeatedly told myself, *I don't deserve to call myself chronically ill* and *I don't need to take time off from school to focus on my health* because I didn't want to.

After MMD, I was sure I was running out of time and needed to keep up at full speed or faster to maximize my time at school. Some nights I would lie awake and have an endless loop ruminating on when the next disease would show up and upheave my life. I had already had two scares less than ten years apart. In that case, I wondered if I had enough or done enough in case my time was going to abruptly stop like it did when I was diagnosed with hypertrophic cardiomyopathy and MMD.

What scared me the most in those silent moments was the numbing realization that no amount of planning or aspiring to whatever I had convinced myself in that moment would make me feel better about the brevity of our existence would be enough.

One of my new favorite authors, Kate Bowler, writes about her diagnosis with a type of cancer that should've been terminal in her book No Cure for Being Human. Bowler explains that there will never be enough moments for her, enough anniversaries, enough hugs, enough moments with her son, or enough time to send her father her thoughts on history books or passages she has read—which is something me and my dad have done since I was seventeen—and so on.

If I give this fire too much oxygen, it's impossible to measure life this way, and "enough" becomes an aversion to living my life. Thinking about "enough" keeps me in the hospital, feeling like I will never recover.

In the movies, when adults are diagnosed with a chronic illness, they quit their job or take time off to reevaluate their values and decisions. They have a midlife crisis.

No Cure for Being Human clarifies how the perception of "enough" habitually centers around if career aspirations are met or if fancy and shiny material things are accumulated. It's rare to see "enough" quantified by love, compassion, hope, or nonmaterial things.

What is the protocol when that happens to a kid? What is the plan when you are so aware of time but in a setting like college that already glorifies reckless decisions and promotes unhealthy habits? I used to quantify "enough" by the structure school had provided me for the last eighteen years. Dedicating enough time and effort awarded me decent grades and opportunities I was terrified to miss. Entertaining the idea of taking a semester off post MMD surgery would've offset my plan to graduate from Syracuse in four years. I naively thought that idea wasn't worth pursuing.

But that semester, I should have called in sick. Looking back, I was in way over my head. I didn't take my parents', close friends', or academic advisors' advice about taking a semester off from school to give myself more time to heal.

My parents left Syracuse, and my sophomore year started off normal—until it wasn't.

My roommate and I lived in an open double, so we spent a lot of time together. Our beds were on opposite sides of a big room from each other, and there was very little privacy. She used to say, "I assumed Emma was either two places if she wasn't in her bed: class or the hospital." Weird thing to say about a kid who is healthy.

The second week of school was the first time I spent time in the hospital sophomore year. I was hospitalized more that year than at any time prior to getting my heart transplant. Even in the first year posttransplant, I was only admitted to the hospital twice. I was in the hospital four times my sophomore year.

It has taken me a while to conclude and be okay with the fact that I don't live the same way now as I did with my heart transplant when I first received it. I fluctuated from being a newly minted recipient, paranoid, about my suppressed immune system—worrying about holding hands with other people to touching a dirty surface and not washing my hands after—to completely ignoring my health and chronic condition when I arrived at college.

As I got older, I developed a deeply rooted anger toward my heart that dictated a lot of my decisions. All I wanted was to be normal and make the same reckless decisions I thought everyone else in college was making: pulling all-nighters, getting drunk all the time, and not worrying about blood draw results, medication refills, or coordinating care between four different doctors in two different states.

My fear of time influenced my decisions based on what I thought I "should" be doing compared to everyone else my age.

I should graduate in four years. I should say yes to all these opportunities offered because I know what it's like to suddenly feel like you are losing all these opportunities to your health. I should use my body until it physically gives out on me so I can get everything out of this college experience before I run out of time. The only way I knew how to be mindful was to overextend myself to extremes. The list could go on for a while, especially after my third hospitalization that year.

I was essentially trying to outrun my body and miserably losing the race.

More than anything, when I lay in those hospital beds, I was tired of fighting my body. I wanted a break from the meds, the chronic pain, and the pressure to have this perfect college experience. I wasn't the only one my frequent visits were affecting, either. My parents got phone calls at all times of the day and night from me and sometimes my friends, downplaying the situation and trying to let my parents know what had happened without worrying them. My parents answered every phone call or text with a plan already made up about how they would get to Syracuse.

It's hard to explain how present and supportive my parents are. Whether it was four in the morning or in the afternoon, they were there. I know if I needed them now, they would still come as fast as they could to support me. I know what a privilege it is to receive this kind of unconditional love and support, and I know that is what parents are for: taking care of their kids. At a certain point, though, I felt bad for the amount of stress I put on them.

I can literally hear my therapist's voice in my head as I am writing this, reminding me I have no control over my medical conditions and it isn't my fault my heart failed. These were the cards dealt to me, and the guilt we are all carrying around is holding us in the past. I know this, and yet, I catch myself feeling this way all the time.

The guilt I carry is heavy, and I try to imagine leaving bits and pieces of it behind as I continue to grapple with how to take care of my body. Still, I felt like such a burden, and I hated that school and life were getting interrupted by dumb hospital stays.

My parents always said, "Our job is to enable you," and their faith in me has carried me all over the world without having to worry about my physical health dictating my life. Mental health, on the other hand, well, that's a different story. They never wanted me to sit at home holding my heart transplant and coddling it.

I should be living my life, and I am because in doing so, my parents taught me to show up for it. My transplant is the reason I can make decisions that don't stick to the prescription of what I think I should be doing but rather what I need to be doing.

NOT EVERYTHING HAPPENS FOR A REASON

Telling me you "don't know how I do it" isn't the compliment you think it is. If this was your body, I am pretty sure you would do the same and learn to feel at home with it.

I am not sure I believe in God or subscribe to one particular denomination, but when I was a kid, I used to sing this song in Hebrew school by Dan Nichols called "B'tzelem Elohim."

"B'tzelem Elohim" is the Hebrew phrase for "in God's image." When we were kids singing in music class, God's image was celebrated by looking around the classroom and talking about how our differences were what made us special. It was the "God made us who we are" and "We're all perfect just the way we are" crap.

Now that I am different, with physical changes to my body, I don't always feel special, and the lyrics of what used to be one of my favorite songs remind me I am not made perfectly. In fact, I have quite a few medical malfunctions. After my transplant, I began to think, *if I was created in God's image, why was I created with faulty parts? How is it fair that God chose me to go on this fucking difficult journey?*

What was the reason for all this happening?

At the beginning of the last decade or so, mainly in those first couple of years posttransplant, many people tried comforting me by saying "everything happens for a reason" and that they were "so sorry for me." Before that, I couldn't pinpoint a time when I held onto such deep-rooted shame.

We were all still stunned with shock posttransplant, and rightfully so. I'm sure people didn't know what to say or how to comfort my parents, Keri, or me when they found out how sick I was and how I had almost died. To be fair, the reflex response to most traumatic situations—like getting that text from a friend about a breakup or the phone call that a family member is sick—is to say, "I am sorry." We want to apologize because it's almost too uncomfortable to put ourselves in the situation our loved one is experiencing. It's easier to say, "I am sorry" and then forget about it.

But every "sorry" and look of pity settled deep in my core. People's sympathy only reminded me that I didn't have this perfect vessel God created. If they felt sorry for me, I should too because why would they say it if they didn't mean it?

The ironic thing about wanting to avoid relating to someone "going through it" is that we are all going through it at some point.

The expectation is we are all designed as these perfect humans and the only time we will experience loss, grief, sadness, anger, disappointment, or fear is after we've lived a long life. Those clichés about the only thing promised in life is death are "cliché" because if we think about them and the truth behind them for too long, their truth is terrifying. We don't talk about the disorder that we all share that makes us believe this illusion that we are immortal, that we are invincible from bad shit happening that may affect our health and change our lives overnight.

In my head, at least, I understood death as something that only happens to old people who are in a nursing home. This illusion is further exacerbated by the commodification of the bullshit "life is good" and "look at the glass half full" mentality.

I was seven years old when I first experienced symptoms of mortality.

I was in the car with my older sister and parents, and we were listening to a James Taylor CD when I had my first anxiety attack. All these years later, it's difficult to pinpoint why that obtrusive thought decided to streak across my brain just as the chorus to "How Sweet It Is" came out of the car speaker. What I do remember, though, is asking my parents, "What happens to us when we die?" That was the first time I conceptualized I would not live forever. My parents might have said something generic along the lines of visiting my great grandparents in heaven or something, but who knows. All I could do was repeat that question over and over again.

What happens to us when we die?

The song ended, and so did the conversation. There was no air in the car, and I was sure the seat belt got tighter and tighter around me. My consciousness of my grounding on Earth dissipated. I was no longer sitting in my booster seat in the car but floating in a black hole. My surroundings were whirling by me as I floated through this dark matter, and planets were orbiting around my floating body. I had no idea where I was.

I tried to fall asleep, to turn off my brain, anything to mute the ringing in my ears and pounding of my chest. How could I prepare for the *end* if no one knew what it was? I needed directions. My heart raced at the time, and my heart transplant was still five years in the future.

Fifteen years later, I wonder if my parents even remember that car ride. After that anxiety attack, before I fell asleep at night, I would say I love you to every family member in my head so if I were to die in my sleep, my last thought would be about loving my family. Tellingly, it was almost like I was preparing for when I woke up in the hospital after my heart transplant.

What was the reason my family had to witness such a scary experience? I am sure while we mostly got through those days, weeks, and months posttransplant, my transplant isn't the reason why my mom is so empathetic or why Keri is an amazing teacher. My family's strength, resilience, and compassion were there before and didn't need a reason to flex these values.

Don't get me wrong. If searching or pinpointing a reason back to an event has helped you heal, who am I to diminish that? My goal is to bring light to a circumstance where that mentality has been harmful. Sometimes, looking for omnipotent meaning in everything can be more harmful than helpful.

It's also fucking exhausting.

I think people offer different versions of the sentiment "everything happens for a reason" because that is what has been said before and it's on a Hallmark card. From the inspirational home decor and cards that tell you to live like every moment is your last, to TV commercials promoting products to make you live longer and look younger, this mentality is embedded in the culture of our society. Everyone wants to live longer, but no one wants to talk about why. We are all afraid of dying. At least I am. And I have come close to dying a few too many times.

For some people, looking at the glass as half full and the "precious moments culture" serves them well. I used to wish I was one of those types of people. I thought of it in a binary way; I was either an optimist or a pessimist, and my glass was always half empty.

The idea I made up in my head is a caricature of some bitchy, whiny human who is ungrateful and hates everything. I kept seeing these signs, even in my own kitchen growing up, that said things like "live like every moment is your last" or "life is not measured by the number of breaths we take, but by the moments that take our breath away" and I wanted to scream because they all made me feel so ridiculous for feeling guilty.

What was wrong with me? Why was I not an optimistic person? Was I a bad person for not buying into this crap?

If I could understand the reason why both my heart and brain needed life-saving surgery then maybe I could prevent it from happening again. I particularly convinced myself that pinpointing a reason would help me better take care of my heart and prove that I am deserving of it. If I knew what symptoms to look out for, I wouldn't let my heart fail again.

I am so traumatized from waking up in that hospital bed completely disoriented that I play mental gymnastics trying to control every aspect of my life, down to how long my heart transplant is going to last. The obstacles in my brain would tick less if I could just grasp the control I crave long enough.

There was no logical reason for my transplant happening. To be frank, it wasn't fair, and I didn't ask for any of this. No one in my family or extended family has ever been diagnosed with hypertrophic cardiomyopathy or had a heart transplant. After my transplant, I even had genetic testing* done to try to understand why this all happened, to make a more educated guess on why my heart had failed, to find a reason.

Still nothing: All the genetic markers came back negative.

The less my family talked about my transplant journey over the years, the less I understood whatever this almighty reason was supposed to be. I couldn't extrapolate specific details from everyday life or accomplishments that would lead to the specific reason, which pissed me off. I was waiting for a package to arrive at my front door from God explaining the whole thing in a short little book with the final chapter confirming I would end up okay.

The thought of coming so close to death still keeps me awake at night, especially because it wasn't until recently that I considered myself chronically ill or disabled. We didn't talk about how we were feeling at home, or how I was feeling, unless I had a doctor's appointment coming up or when family members called and checked in on us. I didn't acknowledge that I was different because in doing so, I had to let go of trying to get better or be cured from something that was never going to go away.

For years after my transplant, I couldn't look in the mirror without a shirt on. I was scared to see my scars and even more ashamed I had them. Shame controlled what I wore, who I talked to, how I carried myself, and who entered the room first: me or my emotional baggage. It infected me, and I brooded in it daily because it was a huge member of my life.

People felt sorry for me, so I felt sorry for myself.

The mental and emotional changes that followed my heart transplant, in comparison to the physical changes in my body, were a greater source of shame by far. Shame because my body is different and therefore needs more support. Shame because we didn't talk about my transplant until years after; therefore, I didn't understand how sick I was, so I didn't treat or think of myself as chronically ill. I thought if people saw my scars, saw who I truly was, then I would be less of a person because of them. Hiding them meant hiding the reason people felt sorry for me. My scars made me imperfect and disqualified me from competing in unobtainable comparisons between me and everyone else I saw on Instagram who seemed perfect. (Brené Brown, TEDx Houston)

I only shared glimpses about my transplant journey at school and was very selective about who got to hear it. In retrospect, that was my irrational way of gaining control over a situation I had had no choice but to surrender to. I tried controlling who heard my story and how. The box I shut myself in not only closed me out but others as well. I made the decision for others that they couldn't handle hearing the stories behind my scars, both physical and metaphorical. I'm sure that came across clear as day to everyone I interacted with at school. I was miserable.

During the summer leading up to my sophomore year of high school, I had the privilege of collaborating with Hearts for Emma and the New Jersey Sharing Network* to make educational materials about organ, tissue, and cornea donation and transplantation. New Jersey was one of the first states in the country to ratify a law promoting the lifesaving benefits of organ, tissue, and cornea donation and transplantation.

The Hero Act requires public high schools, public institutions of higher education, colleges of medicine, and educational programs for professional nursing in the state to educate students on organ and tissue donation as well as create the opportunity for students to become donors if they so choose. (New Jersey Hero Act Summary) However, when I first saw the existing education materials for the Hero Act curriculum, my initial reaction was, *Holy shit, this is me too.* I am a version of the recipients in the video.

At the time, I hadn't confronted my discomfort with identifying as a transplant recipient, and I couldn't connect to the material. Watching it forced me to reconcile with that, and I had a visceral response that was shame driven. Admitting I was similar to the people starring in the video made me feel inferior and want to hide my transplant even more.

Unknowingly, I internalized all that shit deep down—so far down, in fact, that I couldn't find it for years. I was embarrassed by how the video made me feel, and I couldn't imagine others associating my story with that video.

Instead of encouraging students to have lifesaving conversations surrounding organ and tissue donation, registering to become an organ donor, or even on a more serious note, letting your loved ones know your wishes, the video continued to perpetuate the taboo stereotype of transplants.

Yet when I envisioned updated and relatable educational materials, I wasn't the face of them. I wanted to use my voice, but behind the scenes so I didn't have any more attention on me than I already felt like I did or have to acknowledge the fact that the transplant recipient part of me was now who I was.

I tried to be everything, and it was exhausting trying to juggle so many hats—the high school volleyball athlete, the student, the advocate and activist, the nonprofit board member; and that was all without including my chronic illness. Depending on who I was with, I wore whichever hat I made up in my head of what a normal high school person should be. Intending to fit in, I tailored my personality and probably suppressed a lot of shit to fit in with some impossible standard.

I was presented with the opportunity to star in, direct, and refurbish the curriculum (consisting of an educational video and brochure), but my initial, internal reaction wanted to decline the opportunity. I couldn't pay attention to why

I felt so ashamed of the old materials because I lacked the perspective I have now.

I can't wipe my scars away, and no amount of therapy will change what happened the last week of March in 2011.

I said yes, mostly because my survivor's guilt made me feel like I couldn't say no. I joined a production project to make a video about organ and tissue donation but still didn't know completely what had happened to me during my own transplant journey and the fifteen days surrounding it. For the most part, all I understood was my donor's loved ones decided to make a decision which saved my life. I could explain hypertrophic cardiomyopathy, my medications, and how successful and healthy I felt, but that was about it.

That's all anyone wanted to hear, really—how well I was doing—and that was loud and clear to me from most of the interactions I had with parents, friends of parents, past coaches, and medical professionals.

I need to be abundantly clear when I say I don't regret making the video, brochure, or follow-up materials. The "You Have the Power to Save Lives" curriculum has reached over 150,000 high school students in New Jersey since publishing the material. That wouldn't have been possible without the New Jersey Sharing Network, Hearts for Emma, or the support from our community. It's just that I wasn't ready to confront my own discomfort with disability, specifically organ and tissue donation, because to "Try and understand it is to be okay enough with yourself in every stage of growth and being so that you don't see your body as damaged." (*The Pretty One*, Brown) All I saw in the mirror was damage. I wasn't okay with myself.

The damage I saw in the mirror made me feel like less of a person, like I deserved less because of all of my baggage.

The only emotional regulation skill I had at that time was hiding any and all feelings I had about my heart. I felt like a fraud because I didn't know I could feel eternally grateful and less whole as a human at the same time. On the outside, when talking to people, advocating at organ donation and transplantation and blood drive events, getting interviewed, and even talking to my own family, I smothered any feeling other than gratitude and projected what I thought people wanted to see.

Acknowledging I was different, or more importantly, assigning meaning to others acknowledging I was different, meant they too would see me as inferior because in my head, I already saw myself as inferior and damaged. (*The Pretty One*, Brown)

When people tell me everything happens for a reason, I hear and internalize that I have to find meaning from excruciating experiences—because if I don't, then what was the point? It feels like there are these productivity benchmarks to healing, and I am missing them all because I don't have a great answer for the reason for all of this. Instead of trying to find an explanation for things that can't be explained, maybe there should be Hallmark cards that say, "It was not your fault, and you are not defected or any less of a human because of your trauma."

As Dr. Bessel van der Kolk's *The Body Keeps the Score* explains, "Self-blame, and accepting that the trauma is not my fault, that it was not caused by some defect in me, and that I could never have deserved what happened to me," seems more productive than wondering why.

Knowing and believing this, I can confirm that it is still annoyingly difficult.

WHAT THE FUCK DO I KNOW?

Even though we never talked about it, in a way, all four members of my family lost control over how our lives used to be.

I used to think I was the only one who didn't have time to adjust to my new roles or prepare for how my transplant changed so many aspects of our lives, but my mom, dad, and Keri didn't get the time to adjust either.

Every family indeed has their shit that gets swept under the rug or hangs in a photo on the wall; everyone knows it's there, but no one talks about the feelings behind the smiling portraits. For a long time, my transplant was that for my family, and in some ways, it still is.

Therapy played a huge role in learning that in those moments of remembering our swept-away secret, my relationship with my heart was at its worst, and in turn, the relationships around me suffered. Taking care of my heart transplant in the beginning without consistently seeing a therapist was like an extracurricular event on top of school and all the other activities I was involved in. I had no energy for anything else but maintaining those responsibilities.

Turns out, what I thought was rock bottom in high school while working with Amy, a local therapist, was only a taste of the shit college threw at me.

Even though past therapists who treated me were not versed in the medical world, they did validate that the hurricanes I had braved were, in fact, anxiety attacks. I needed to hear that I wasn't making shit up in my head. Even though no one in my family was talking about my transplant or how it affected them, my experience in the hospital was enough to qualify me as an anxious person, but not yet a chronically ill person. That came way later.

The distinction of my chronic anxiety diagnosis relieved so much internal pressure because I had convinced myself for so long that I was making more of a big deal about how the chronicity of my transplant affected me than it actually was. Anxiety was for people who were sick enough or had gone through tough enough shit—not for me.

When I was Amy's patient, the only part of my story I knew was that my heart had failed and I had woken up with a transplant. I had picked up other details here and there and wasn't really looking for more clarification, and I did as much as I could to separate myself from my transplant, both internally and externally. I wanted to leave my transplant in the past and, ideally, never look back.

I was terrified to question or speak my truth because it was uncharted territory.

What would she think of me if I told her I would've rather not had the transplant if it meant the survivor's guilt I was feeling over surviving my transplant would subside? What would she think of me if I told her I didn't want my transplant most days? What would she think of me if I told her how I felt about our sessions?

Instead of leaving class at the same time every day in high school to take my meds, I opted to change my medication dose time to 7:30 in the morning to avoid making a scene while getting pulled from class. I gave up precious time in bed to take my meds because the notion of having my transplant take up more space, more of my identity, was something I wasn't willing to let happen. I actively tried to minimize and fight it.

I saw how my transplant impacted my other family members and had no idea how to exist with them as this new person with a chronic illness.

My family had tried family therapy right after my transplant, but it had made things worse. The safe space was abused and turned into a mental boxing ring where the fighting wasn't contained to the office, and it led to spiteful conversations at home.

It hadn't always been like that. When we were kids, Keri and I used to have sleepovers together and sneak chocolates upstairs from my parents' secret stash. She had a trundle bed where we hid the wrappers and other things we weren't supposed to have. Of course, the chocolate melted everywhere, and being the cool older sister she was, she used to flip the blankets over to hide the stains while I had a panic attack that we were going to get in trouble.

We stayed up all night laughing and playing games until my dad came in and yelled at us to go to bed because we were too loud. We spent a lot of time together. It was the kind of relationship where my parents are just finding out about the shenanigans we got up to as kids.

As Keri got older, most days after school, she was the babysitter until I had my transplant and my mom stopped working to take care of me. This was why the transition of our relationship was so confusing to me, after my transplant when everything changed; I thought our relationship would be the one constant.

My relationship with Keri became screaming at each other from across the house.

We fought about everything, from mindless shit like steal-ing each other's shirts to hurling insults at each other when there was a misunderstanding—usually when anything to do with my transplant came up. Nothing I said was what she wanted to hear, and our fights always somehow came back to my transplant: How I was the favorite child and got everything I wanted (posttransplant), or how insensitive I was to others' feelings. Normal conversations turned bloody really quickly over the littlest things.

Her biggest punch was, "You are only getting that because of your heart transplant and because people feel bad for you." That bruise is still healing. It was hard not to internalize her reaction. After all, Keri's my big sister, and if she said it, there had to be some truth behind it. Every accomplishment from then on felt like a scam because the accolade wasn't for me; it was for the thing that had happened to me, as if without my transplant, I wouldn't be smart enough or as hardworking.

I tied my self-worth to accomplishing things, but when I did accomplish things, Keri's voice in my head triggered a self-deprecating response.

I let it dictate how I felt about myself for a long time.

In my second year of college after my second brain surgery, I started seeing Dr. J., a clinical psychologist, and my com-forting, redemptive transplant script went out the window.

We started from scratch.

I had barely gotten over my therapeutic breakup from my last therapist when I found myself sitting in Dr. J.'s office three times a week. The last time I sat on a therapist's couch, I was a seventeen-year-old high school student. After hour-long sessions with Amy, I left her office fuming and often came home and sat in my bathtub and cried. My emotions had full control over me, and they were so intense that if I wasn't sitting in the tub—a safe secure space—I was afraid of passing out.

Week after week was the same thing: sit on Amy's blue couch clutching the box of Kleenex, hoping it would anchor me. During those sessions, I would've rather been anywhere else than sitting on her couch. Letting my thoughts wander felt safer than sitting with what I was feeling in the moment.

But when I got to Dr. J.'s office, there was no couch or weird motivational stock art hanging on the wall. My mom drove with me to the appointment, and I remember having the talk with her: "I'll be right outside if you need me. Remember, you don't have to commit to anything. Just give it a shot." I had heard this before and just nodded my head. I was already trying to take mental notes to prepare for the session. When Dr. J. came out in the waiting room to get me, I was thrown off by how young she was. In my mind, therapists were moms or old ladies like in the movies, and she looked a little older than Keri.

I wasn't sleeping at the time and went a few days only getting a couple of hours of uninterrupted sleep. My anxiety about something going wrong with my body and dying in my sleep kept me awake. Reoccurring nightmares of floating in space were no longer happening only during anxiety attacks but nightly when I tried to sleep. I couldn't stop my mind from wandering to that scary place.

And after my experience with Amy, I had a tainted taste of therapy and was sure that whatever Dr. J. thought she could do wouldn't work. So for Dr. J.'s first encounter with me, I was sleep-deprived, in pain, and agitated. I am sure I looked like a walking zombie because I felt like a shell of a human. My eyes were still so sensitive to light from the surgery that we met in the dark, yet it was still a very impactful session.

At the end of our session, Dr. J. looked me in the eye and straight up asked me if I wanted to work with her. My face turned red, and I remember stuttering because no one had asked before what I wanted, especially not in a medical setting. Dr. J. immediately gave me the autonomy to "steer the ship," as she says. During the first session, she told me that her style of therapy was like the first mate on a ship. They help guide the captain, but ultimately the captain is the one turning the wheel, making the decisions, and driving the boat north with the help of the crew.

This time, when I got in the car after the session, I wasn't fuming, jumping out of my skin, or even crying. I got in the car fairly calmly, and I appreciated my mom not peppering me with questions that I couldn't yet answer myself. I had a lot to process.

Dr. J. mentioned things I had never heard about in a therapeutic setting, or ever; cognitive behavioral therapy (CBT),* pain management without using pain medications, and using values to make decisions instead of my raging emotions. In only a few minutes, I had started to unravel, and my hesitations about therapy started to dissolve. Her straightforwardness was refreshing and relatable. I had yet to meet someone who mirrored my candidness and even challenged me, especially during our first forty-minute encounter. She also gave me homework from the first session, which was probably the first time I rolled my eyes at her; it didn't take too long.

When I met Dr. J., I had less than two weeks at home left before I moved back to college in Syracuse to start my sophomore year. We met three times a week to establish a relationship, and during those first six sessions, never once did I have to explain a procedure, how hospital life worked, or even explain Hearts for Emma. Dr. J. had done her homework too, and she worked in a pediatric and adult neurology center at a hospital.

While I did explain some medications and the implications of test results, we started with a shared general knowledge of what my life revolved around, which made a lifesaving difference. This meant we got to start putting in the work right away. My fear of losing time and perfectionist tendencies energized me to lean into therapy. I was going to get an A in this class.

Originally, I thought therapy would only be a fall semester class. We would work together, and then in the new year, she would discharge me as her patient. Dr. J. would give me all the answers I needed that I wasn't capable of finding, and I would be back to enabling myself to live my life to its fullest.

That was the furthest thing from the truth.

It's annoying how good Dr. J. is at her job. Every time I ask what she thinks or what to do for fear of making a mistake, she is quick to guide me back to myself. Isn't she the expert? As I continued to devote time to myself during Dr. J.'s sessions, we uncovered how my transplant affected each of my family members differently. That one experience isn't more valid than the other, although in the beginning, I naively thought my experience was the most traumatic and therefore the most valid.

I was stuck in my pigeonhole and as Dr. J. would say, letting my emotions lead in the driver's seat. I was the one who was going to have to live with this shit every day; Keri and our parents had the option to turn it off if they wanted to, or in Keri's case, move out of the house and go to college. She wasn't the one who needed to take pills for the rest of her life, coordinate her health care, or have routine procedures because of a transplant.

That pissed me off. How could she be so mean to me when she was healthy? Her body worked and functioned, and she was mad at me for separating our family like I had a choice or asked for all of that attention. Every fight between Keri and my mom, or me and my mom, felt like my fault. If I hadn't gotten sick, maybe Keri wouldn't have felt so neglected by my parents, or maybe my family would've been more cohesive if my transplant hadn't happened.

The older I am, the less I remember about pretransplant life, so it was easy to believe her. After all, she's my sister. I couldn't understand why she would say those things if she didn't mean them. In the midst of this battleground, no one was listening to each other, and all we were doing was reacting to our own pain.

I didn't think it was possible for my parents or Keri to be in as much pain as I was. Sure, the start of my journey was traumatic, but since I didn't know most of it, I had little idea what they went through and had a difficult time empathizing with their experience.

I still will never be able to understand what it was like to see me so unstable with little to no certainty that my body would make it before doctors decided that a transplant was the last option. I used to think I was the only one in pain and upset by how it all played out, but my other family members were also affected, just differently.

Those fights are hard to let go of, even though they were so long ago, because Keri and I intentionally tried to hurt each other, whether we admitted it to ourselves or not. As a younger sister, I couldn't and still can't understand what Keri took on as my big sister the day I got sick. I thought I was the only one who had to grow up overnight, but she was just a kid too.

As much as I wanted to perfect therapy, there was an even stronger pull that dragged me to the floor. My good fucking friend depression led me to a new, deep, rock-fucking-bottom. I was lying on the floor of my college dorm sobbing through the phone to some person I had met only a few months ago about how I wasn't sure I was going to make it through sophomore year.

The same anxiety attacks I experienced when I was seven were now happening daily: in the library, during class, out at a party on the weekend where I soberly followed my friends around, trying to reason why anyone thought this was what the college experience was supposed to be like. I felt like an alien in my own skin and in the college world. The scars from my brain surgery were still itchy from healing, and I had no idea why I was at school.

Weeks ago, I had just had my second health crisis, and I was spending my precious time doing mindless busywork assignments and dancing in smelly frat house basements. What the actual fuck was I doing? Was this how I wanted to use my 86,400 precious seconds of every day that I would never get back?

Obviously, I didn't have any of these answers, and Dr. J. refused to give me answers. Her job is apparently to only help with my journey, she says, not the destination. Fuck the destination if the journey is also miserable and you make the wrong decision and waste even more time.

Sometimes I genuinely tried to convince her why I overextended myself for something I thought I should be doing and was acting on my anxiety about missing out on opportunities, and other times, I just lay there and cried because I didn't know what else to do. Seeing her weekly is one of the few times I feel safe and comfortable digging into the last ten years.

I am not worried about saying the wrong thing or stepping on eggshells to try to keep the peace between my family because it's me time. For the entire hour, I am the focus and can listen to my body without feeling guilty or shame for taking the time to pause. This pause I am learning how to respect is saving my life. The pause is giving me a chance to acknowledge how I feel and then, ideally, on a good day, decide if it's worth my time or if I value it enough to act on it.

Pausing allowed me to realize how violated I felt from all the medical procedures. My body has been cut, pricked, and poked so many times that it's difficult to feel whole inside my skin.

Honestly, the last two and a half years Dr. J. and I have worked together, my relationship to therapy has not always been cordial. No matter how many times I flipped her off or rolled my eyes at her because there was no way she could possibly understand what being so aware of your own mortality feels like, she challenged me and mirrored just as much attitude back.

Session after session became more draining than the previous one, and I often wanted to give up on my healing journey. To my surprise, uncovering and processing trauma is an uncomfortably long process that doesn't have a syllabus or time frame. My transplant is never going away, and neither are my pills or the aggravations I have with being chronically ill.

I want to decide how I am touched and when, and there is no shame in that. Working with Dr. J. helped me realize that doctors stripped a lot of my body autonomy from me without much warning. They made these decisions for me based on test results and biometric needs, not on my feelings toward being afraid of blood draws or being tired of echocardiograms.

Of course, had I been awake and capable of making the decision to undergo surgery, I would've chosen my transplant without a doubt. I just would've appreciated being present when that conversation was first brought up and ultimately when the decision was made to list me on the registry.

I learned the hard way that even worse than not being given advice is sitting in silence. Despite craving control, I was desperate to be told what to do, which college major to decide on, what I should do over the weekend, how to handle a family fight, or how I should feel about anything that happened that week because I was terrified, and to some degree still am, of making a mistake and wasting some of my nonrefundable time. Really, I was just terrified to trust myself.

Although I am learning to find validation within myself and expect it from no one other than me, I still often need reminders and consciously put in work to unlearn the feelings and habits I have around validation.

What I didn't know then is I have a right to feel however the fuck I want to, and that is for me and only me. Depriving myself of the space to feel and express my vulnerable, unfiltered thoughts isn't what my doctor meant when she told me that my transplant should enable me to live my best life.

I no longer expect my parents or Keri to understand me, which alleviates a lot of the pressure from our relationship.

It had never occurred to me just how much time my parents and I spent together in the car, driving back and forth from the city, or resting for days or weeks after some tough medical visits.

I resented that we spent so much of our time taking care of me; I will never earn that time back. I even felt guilty for being so aware of how precious time is and having to spend it in the car or in waiting rooms when I know my attitude was less than pleasant to be around. One of the first times I spent continuous alone time with my parents, not in our home or doing medical shit, was about seven years posttransplant.

There is now space for reconnecting and creating new memories and inside jokes that don't orbit around the hospital.

That is the thing about time: the score rarely is even, and there is never enough of it. I am still waiting, honestly expecting, some big aha moment when suddenly I will be cured from the depression and uncomfortable feelings surrounding my transplant.

But for now, I am still showing up for myself during our weekly sessions because I am the only one that is going to save myself from my own reality.

WHAT IS ENOUGH?

It was easy to be at war with my body constantly. My brain tries to overpower my body with what it is realistically capable of without overextending.

Ideally, I wanted to do it all without paying attention to what my body needed because paying attention meant pausing. Pausing is the antonym of maximizing every day. Giving in and taking the time I needed to rest meant admitting defeat versus overextending my body and ending up in the hospital multiple times a year during college. This war consumed my time and became impossible to balance.

If you had asked me what I wanted most ten years ago, I would've regurgitated something I had heard or read from other transplant recipients like, "Living my life to its fullest." This is what outsiders looking in expect to hear from transplant recipients, so I didn't think to say anything else. Who wanted to hear about the struggles that happened behind the scenes of trying to live life with a transplant as a twenty-something?

There would've been no introspective questioning or second thought as to what living life to its fullest meant, or more importantly, what it meant to *me*.

Living life to its fullest is an umbrella term for all the moments in between the narrative surrounding transplants that are omitted most of the time. Rarely do you read about the number of bruises, scars, and wounds recipients have from countless procedures.

Is that what it looks like to live life to its fullest? Often feeling like a human pincushion for IVs and blood draw sticks? While those procedures enable me to live, I can think of a million other things that would be more fulfilling than throwing up for ten hours post-op or getting fifteen vials of blood drawn.

When I was in the organ donation and transplantation environment at the beginning of the decade, it was mostly adult-centered. I heard their wisdom by the way they talked about their transplant and mirrored what they said. Most of my friends in the community are double my age or older than my parents' age. There weren't many kids I could relate to, both in school and at transplant events. The way we talk about transplants has dramatically changed within the last ten years and continues to change as more information is widely available and the societal acceptance of discussing taboo topics becomes the norm through various social media channels Instagram wasn't a common platform yet back then, and TikTok wasn't even on the horizon.

All transplant experiences are different. However, the age gap didn't work in my favor because they were at such different life stages when they got sick or when they had their surgery or how long they had been on the path of recovery. Their perspective included years of experience and tools they'd learned throughout their life, which was probably the optimism I lacked. At times, it became easier to relate and connect with sixty and seventy-year-olds than with my friends at school.

When people used to ask me what happened, I had to defer to my parents. I spoke through them because I didn't have the confidence, or knowledge, until I was ready to discuss my narrative with my parents to answer their questions.

I felt a lot of shame in that.

People often want to read about the struggle. They are curious about it, and then they want to indulge in how you overcame it. Stories that end nicely and neatly are motivating; their struggle eventually ended, and yours can too. This isn't to say that the narratives published and spoken in the transplant community aren't genuine or true. It just felt like they weren't as authentic as I would expect them to be, being a transplant recipient myself. But I argue that sometimes those illnesses, obstacles, or whatever hardships that impact day-to-day living sometimes cannot be overcome, and that is okay.

When we fail to talk about these moments, any experience that is less than magical feels wrong and shameful. My shame because of that entered the room before I did, and it was difficult to sit with it and even more difficult to talk about.

These moments can be ugly and are probably not shared for a reason. I am asking that we create space in the transplant community that is more inclusive and mindful of all the moments that make up our narratives, not just the pretty "living life to its fullest" moments. Because living life to its fullest, for me at least, is the power and capability to feel all these things and know that I got myself through them. I'm more interested in that than only talking about the glorifying parts.

Our culture loves the dream that anyone can overcome anything to achieve success, but this dream only fits one persona: an able-bodied go-getter. The structure that I grew up in, all the way through college, socialized me to intertwine worthiness and productivity—that I was only successful and worthy if I were actively contributing to society.

Whether this dream refers to success or the means of achieving success, both ideologies are harmful.

If you can't get over your disability or receive a cure for it, you're excluded from the definition of success and are only useful as a warning of what your life could be like. *(The Pretty One*, Brown) I am sure this is common for a lot of people, but since I was a kid, I was told by family members, mentors—you name it—to reach for the moon and stars because the clouds will catch me if I fail. That is an over-romanticized way of promoting horrible expectation management.

In my experience, it's really hard to have an invisible disability in this overachiever environment because all I wanted to do was pass as normal. I glorified the idea of not having anything wrong with my body. I wanted to be just another person going after their dreams or whatever silly thing I told myself I needed to achieve to maximize my life. But I'll say it; passing as normal is fucking exhausting.

For most of my time at college, I felt like I was running this race against my peers but I had started way after they did and I was moving in slow motion, trying to grasp onto my surroundings and simultaneously keep up with my friends. I never caught up.

At times, passing made it more difficult to fit in, which was the original motivation to suppress and downplay how sick I was to my friends or even the reason why I needed my transplant in the first place. Ignoring my body, in service of not wanting to deal with my chronic illness, did more physical and mental damage because I got sick more often. Every sick day or hospitalization felt like a missed opportunity, and I felt guilty for needing time to heal, time away from school, and time away from the structure I thought was the center of my being. My sick days tend to be a lot different from those of people with all of their original body parts intact, but I refused to accept that.

I convinced myself that my academic disability accommodations were a crutch to help me cheat this dream that I thought everyone was going after.

At the beginning of every semester, meeting with my disability adviser was such a chore because in my head, I didn't see myself as disabled or chronically ill. I told myself repeatedly that I didn't need extra time for assignments or absentee waivers because I should be cured. I didn't appear sick in the classroom and didn't feel actively sick often, so it was effortless to forget the times I was hospitalized for putting school over my health.

My idea of maximization has led to many therapy sessions because I literally can't keep up with the standards I set for myself. My body and mind are constantly fighting each other. My body values rest and needs it, but my mind needs to be productive and constantly achieve something.

There are some days, weeks even, where Dr. J. and I talk about setting mini goals for myself, like brushing my teeth twice a day or getting out of bed before noon if I didn't have class, and now, if I don't have work. I am only comfortable with setting goals where the bar is set up in space; anything less than that is a waste of time. I am comfortable mentally berating myself when I don't meet those expectations. Rather than reasonable goal setting, my high-functioning anxiety makes me feel even shittier than I did before about not meeting my goals.

Sometimes, even when I am in bed, my mind is moving, thinking of ways I can continue to squeeze every last moment of this gift given to me to reach the living life to its fullest expectation.

Getting rid of the bar is okay if that's what you need. Most days, I do. The bar ignores my chronic illness and needs. The bar is set for perfection until the time comes when I wear myself out and can't get out of bed from the mental exhaustion of managing all of this. It's incredibly difficult to sit still with the pressure of perfection weighing down on me, even though that is what I need most—stillness.

Recently, Dr. J. and I debated the meaning of the word "maximize."

My biased, inflexible argument was thar living life to its fullest meant saying yes to every opportunity and setting my expectation bar in the stars; that was how I was going to "get everything out of this life" before the ticking time bomb in my chest exploded. Maximizing my time meant using that time to prove that I could do all of these things, even with the chronic aftereffects of having heart and brain surgery.

I didn't know of any other ways to not only prove that I could do all these things but also that I was deserving of this lifesaving gift. My heart transplant and the guilt of never being able to pay my donor family back managed my time.

In reality, everyone's running out of time.

Nobody knows how fast it will go. I am not the only one that is "grappling with the simultaneous length and brevity of our existence," as Bowler vulnerably explained in her book *No Cure for Being Human.*

Dr. J. challenged my perception of maximizing with a question I couldn't answer. "When have you been able to complete your sky-high expectations and continue to do so for more than a couple of days?" She evidently didn't get where I was coming from. "Can you have a quality of life at 95 percent?

What would even 90 percent look like? Are you still able to make values-based decisions and connect with others without burning yourself out?"

At that moment, I was looking for validation, and she met me with a challenge. I craved confirmation and reassurance that I was living my life correctly and that I was following directions.

I knew she was right.

I rolled my eyes and flipped her off because I couldn't answer that question. I would've rather sat in silence than admit she was right about my expectation management. She followed up with another dagger, "How is this serving you? Does everything always have to be black and white?" Obviously not.

Saying yes meant I was not wasting any time because I thought the flip side of doing everything was doing nothing, and if I was doing nothing, then I might as well be dead.

I now know thinking that way was a little inflexible, and before Dr. J. pointed out my fear of not doing or being enough, I only saw things in black and white. It was either enough or not enough, healthy or dying, meeting all my health goals or staying in bed all day and never moving again.

Mentally torturing myself became a habit; I should be eating vegetables because it's good for my heart, but I also love ice cream sandwiches. But if I have ice cream, I am not taking care of my body, which can be bad for my heart. Ice cream is synonymous with a lot of things. I felt a scale on my shoulders weighing me down about if the decision I had made was going to maximize the longevity and health of my heart transplant.

Going to court for every little decision wasn't sustainable, and Dr. J. helped me realize that "enough" could be in the gray area. "Enough" could look one way today and a different way tomorrow. The gray area is messy, and I am comfortable keeping things in neat boxes: black or white.

All these readjustments really started my sophomore year of college. The same year I started working with Dr. J., I was sitting in the hospital and had just received confirmation that I was going to need brain surgery. Knowing what was going to happen was a foreign experience for me. There was freedom in not knowing or being part of the decision-making process for my heart care.

Losing that control, regardless of whether the decision was between life and death, I couldn't take as much autonomy over that decision. I had a day job controlling my thoughts to make up for all that I lost when my body decided to give out on me. I tortured myself up until I started meeting with Dr. J., thinking, *two life-threatening diagnoses within seven years: Someone in the universe is definitely trying to tell me something.*

I had healed for the most part from the surgery and went to college two weeks after. If I took time off from school to give my body more time to heal, I would've had to accept the condition of my mental and physical health. Every moment that I wasn't in school getting closer to my dream job was a moment wasted. I couldn't have even told you what my dream job was then, or now, for a matter of fact; regardless, I needed to stay on track.

Like a ticking time bomb, my anxiety made my heart feel like it was going to blow up at any second.

Even though I am aware of how unrealistic maximizing all aspects of my life is, the less busy I was or the more time I dedicated to putting my needs first, the guiltier I felt and the faster the time bomb would tick. My grandma tells me,

"The older you get, the faster the world spins." Yet I haven't mastered multitasking—actively listening to myself and doing what I think is necessary to maximize my time. My self-talk reminded me daily that I didn't deserve to do things for myself because investing in myself was a waste of time; I should be doing things to honor my donor.

I am still learning to take care of myself. I need to be still. Within the stillness, there is an opportunity to check in with myself and listen to my body and not the spinning. If done right, pausing silences the spinning.

An "after transplant" story is not usually going to detail the journey or process of how each person in the organ donation and transplantation community manages their expectations or balances between being a recipient and living for themselves. A few sentences aren't enough to address the complete picture of the ups and downs of receiving or donating organs and tissues. There isn't enough room for all the complexity and growing pains of coming to terms with who you are as a chronically ill person now and who you were before all of this happened. Neither is there time to address the survivor's guilt and self-imposed pressure to perfectly take care of this miraculous gift you were given.

It's unimaginable to verbalize the feeling of sharing anatomy and fingerprints with another human that you have never met, never will meet, and is dead. Receiving the gift of life also means receiving everything else that comes along with living. It's effortless to believe that everyone is feeling like a grateful, positive ray of sunshine 24–7 because that is what we are exposed to in society, especially where survivors of trauma, or those overcoming major obstacles, are concerned. Everyone wants to see the success stories, even those of us living these supposed success stories.

I am still working on acknowledging that this is the only body I have. It's easier on some days than others, but if I continue to run myself to the ground going one hundred miles per hour, I am going to miss out on something that I value the most—connection. Without connection, all that I love has no meaning.

When I find myself stuck in another hole, surrounded by my fear of death or not doing enough in my lifetime, any decision I make starts with "I should...because I feel..." not "I value...and therefore I am going to...." Feeling scared won't get me any closer to valuing the present moment or seeking opportunities that align with my value of connecting with people.

I can be a success story, but it's truly up to me to know what "living life to the fullest" means for my own life.

THE THING ABOUT ACCEPTING THE LOVE YOU THINK YOU DESERVE

For most of the past ten years, I hated my body. I never took the time to get comfortable with my new body—scars, bruises, rashes, and bumps—or grieve what I had lost.

They were a reminder of everything I was trying to avoid.

I didn't feel comfortable about how I looked in most bathing suits meant for people my age or any low-cut shirts because they were a glaring reminder of what I'd been through, that my body isn't perfect. When my scars are out, I can no longer pass. The scars belonged to all the time I spent in the hospital, and it angered me that they were there in the first place. *What was the reason for this?*

Just when I start to flirt with being comfortable in my own skin again, the fragility of my health reminds me how hard it is to love myself and to accept myself for what and who I am.

Building a mental and physical structure that can withstand constant pivots in my body's health is fucking hard. Over the last ten years, multiple health scares have reinforced the difficult truth that a transplant is not a cure but a second chance to try to make sense of it all. There is nothing that makes me feel more fragile than that statement.

I assumed that my medical fragility was the reason for putting everyone on edge for most of the past decade. I thought if it weren't for my heart transplant, maybe there would be less fighting or if we had time to adjust to our new normal, maybe the four of us would've had an easier time communicating with each other.

Talking about how I felt didn't always feel safe at home when Keri and I lived together at the very beginning of it all. We both were reeling from different painful memories without the knowledge, patience, or skills to talk or actively listen to each other. Advocating for myself brought even more attention to me, which triggered more arguments. I didn't want to accept that I needed it and relied on my parents' help and other resources that I would've never been aware of if it weren't for the transplant. I perceived relying on my parents help, or anyone's for that matter, as being needy.

In my defense, the stigma around being needy, whether in a medical or personal context, is intrinsically negative and disproportionately used as a label for people who identify as a woman. Calling someone needy is not the kind of compliment you'd want to receive under those circumstances. Women are socialized to provide for others and not ask for things. When you have a chronic disease, asking and advocating become an essential medication in maintaining your health.

In certain aspects of my life, I have to be very needy to stay healthy. This looks like follow-up calls and emails that may seem like I am annoying the receptionist when in reality, this is what taking proactive care of myself looks like; needing to know the results of an MRI; or needing to schedule an appointment and calling back however many times are needed until it's scheduled.

This type of needy is lifesaving.

Out of necessity, I have trained myself to unlearn that subconscious idea of needy. I talk to myself over and over again that I am not being annoying by asking the same question until I understand the answer or need reassurance that I am doing okay. That is the medical professional's job, and I can't expect myself to know it all. Although I hate the word self-care, it's almost like that is my version of self-care, where I grant myself a free pass on being needy.

Yet in my experience, advocating for myself has not always gone too well. Why would I want to subject anyone else to the reality of living with a transplant if I wasn't always comfortable doing it in my own home?

I saw the way my medical shit affected my family, and that greatly discouraged me from asking for what I needed outside of our home. It often resulted in fighting with Keri, being told I can't do something, or me feeling like I'm high maintenance and a burden because of the things that I need to be healthy.

Feeling like a burden to someone, whether it be a partner, friend, group, or school, is a universally shitty feeling. I already felt like I didn't deserve to identify as chronically ill because people can't readily see my scars, so in a way, advocating for my needs was exposing that I needed help because of my heart transplant. That neediness fed off my internal shame about my chronic illness. How I looked, how I chose to show up, or how I didn't hindered a lot of my relationships, and sometimes still do.

No one wants to need anything because needing is annoying and vulnerable and messy, right?

I barely felt comfortable sharing that burden with Dr. J. during sessions, let alone a romantic partner. That weight was something I thought I had to carry on my own. I felt bad for relying on my parents so much and didn't want to have to rely on others when my health was going to inevitably fluctuate.

That was before I met Nick.

I was so sure that no one else could love me, scars and all, because I didn't. We have exposure to different variations of "if you can't love yourself, no one can" or "accept the love you think you deserve," and I believed for a long time I didn't deserve Nick or my donor's love.

The connotation around the word "deserve" is similar to "should." Any word on the other side of "deserve" is a binary: one or the other. *I didn't deserve my transplant, and I should be grateful, but...* Deserving usually involves working toward something that is a fixed target, like a scholarship or job promotion. When there is no way to work or earn the word "deserve" and the framework isn't an essay application but your life, how can you measure if you deserve it or not? I was convinced that my transplant made me a lesser person who is not deserving of this love from me—or anyone.

All the walls I thought I had built to protect myself were not Nick-proof. All of a sudden, these core beliefs I had ingrained were being challenged by someone who chose to be in my life. Nick made up his mind, no matter how many times I tried to dismiss him or selfishly made the decision for him that I am not worthy of his love.

The thought of letting someone in scared me; I knew how shitty I felt about myself, what if they also felt that way? I construed reasons why Nick shouldn't love me and tried to convince him that our relationship wouldn't work.

Nick deserves better.

Thoughts like *Nick should be with someone who doesn't need to wake up to three alarms every morning to take meds on time or someone who isn't waiting for their body to fail them again* were at the core of my internal arguments. Spending time with me are minutes he is never going to get back, and I was so aware of that when we first met. I didn't want him wasting his precious time on me.

I wanted to heal or be cured before ever falling in love fully so when I hoped to open myself up to someone, I would feel whole first. There wouldn't need to be an explanation for all the medical shit and the things about it that made me feel broken. I didn't want to deal with it on most days and convinced myself that I didn't want anyone else to either. Talking about your medical needs is not sexy and looks nothing like the relationships I saw in the movies, on TV, or heard about in school. Dr. J. still gets a laugh out of that one. She jokes I'd spend the rest of my life alone if I continued to use that as my excuse.

I had been in relationships before, some stronger than others, but since I spent so much time hating myself and fearing the future, I truly believed I would die young. In turn, I didn't expect much from those relationships, whether long-term or silly interactions, because investing in them seemed pointless. I internalized that investing in relationships was a waste of time because I wasn't going to be around long enough for it to be worthwhile for the other person.

Isolating was easier than putting myself out there because I feared what people thought of me. Making that decision for others was an act of self-defense. My shame decided I wasn't worthy of love because of all the shit that my body was keeping the score on as Dr. van der Kolk mentions in *The Body Keeps the Score*.

My ego worried about one small gust further destroying any amount of self-worth I had left. Feeling loved and wanted was for whole people, and so far, I only felt that kind of unconditional support from my parents, and they have to love me. Anyone else is consciously choosing to know all of me. I used to feel this crippling guilt that the more I invested in partners, and liked them, the more I'd be shortchanging them because I couldn't be this "normal girl" stereotype I had conjured.

I already got a second chance at life, and it's absolutely terrifying to want more—or even scarier, to go after it. *Wouldn't that be selfish of me?*

I should've been out of time, and it made sense to accept that. Operating on borrowed time, from someone else, makes it hard to promise a future. While I hear Dr. J.'s voice in my head normalizing the idea that no one can guarantee a future any more than I can, my stubborn fucking ego likes to think I'm a special exception because of my childhood. In my mind, making it to college was a reach, and now that I have graduated from college, I'm waiting for the day my heart is going to fail again.

That's the fucked-up thing about "being traumatized. It means continuing to organize your life as if the trauma [will continuously reoccur]." (*The Body Keeps the Score,* van der Kolk) The only value I saw in me was my ticking heart-clock; I was waiting for the other shoe to drop.

My insecurities didn't leave much of my psyche untouched. I was familiar with picking apart all the things I never wanted to talk about with anyone, Nick especially. However, I knew I needed to if I wanted to have a healthy relationship and keep Nick in my life. When Nick and I first started spending time together, I found myself sobbing on the floor of his room a lot. The floor was the safest and fastest way to ground myself when I found my head spinning from anxiety. My body didn't know how to react to the emotional safety he provided.

I was mad at myself for falling for him when relationships weren't for me. If that indicates anything about my self-worth, it's that I made those decisions for others before they had a chance to decide for themselves. A relationship meant relying on someone, and I already had that with my donor. Depending on someone so deeply was another score I couldn't make even or gift that I couldn't repay.

Grasping onto all of this was the only way I knew how to identify myself: this messy, fucked-up person with so much baggage. In her book, *The Pretty One*, Brown talks about forgiving herself in service of who she is becoming, and when I read that, it was as if she was talking directly at me. To free myself for new relationships, I needed to seriously work on creating distance from the shame and expectations that I had set for myself. Punishing myself because of my survivor's guilt and lack of control is not exactly honoring my donor the way I intend to.

It will always be a work in progress: expanding my cognitive flexibility to acknowledge my donor and still allow myself to experience joy in all forms, not just with Nick.

WHAT I WANT WANTS ME

Recently, I went on a trip to Hawai'i and spent part of my summer living on a farm with my close friends. The only purpose of the trip was to have fun and celebrate making it through four years of college.

Secretly, it was also to prolong my time before becoming an adult and entering real life post graduation. Unsurprisingly, I had a really hard time letting go of most of the things I used to measure my productivity and validation like grades, accolades, and constant feedback from professors. These were all ways I amounted to using this precious gift given to me.

To my surprise, my depression and anxiety followed me to paradise, and I was fucking pissed that I couldn't slow down without actively trying to organize my life or cure myself of my depression. I wanted so desperately to heal that I tried to come up with directions and a process to answer the most ambiguous question: *What do I want?*

What is next?

That is a tough question for anyone to answer, particularly when you're living through someone else. I'd like to say I came up with a career plan during the month and a half I was there, but instead, I met a shaman—classic island story.

The universe was screaming at me, and I wasn't paying attention to the message until I went to dinner with David. David is the type of person you meet and wonder if he's lived a couple of lives. The day we met him, my friends and I decided that the best way to prepare was arriving at the restaurant in matching hats we had bought an hour before dinner along with a six-pack.

I had the honor of sitting next to David and don't remember what I ate or what I ordered. I was so captivated by him. At first, it was surface-level conversation about what I studied at school, how working on the farm was going, but then one of my friends brought up my heart transplant, and David and I were no longer exchanging small talk.

The conversation shifted.

"I could tell you wanted to share something with me. You are sitting with something," he commented without knowing anything about me other than what my friend had just shared.

In response, I word vomited the last ten years in about three minutes. The weather in Hawai'i became an irrelevant subject, and our questions about each other started to begin with "why" instead of "what." Why was I really at the farm? Why was I torturing myself with this guilt? Our conversation consumed me, yet it concerned my biggest triggers—death and what grieving looks like—while drinking margaritas.

While I paused to catch my breath, David replied, "So I'm assuming what I'm feeling is the guilt you're carrying with your presence. That burden, that load on yourself, is entering the room before you do. And it's taking up so much space, Emma." He rubbed a brown pouch filled with rocks as he shared his observation with me. The noise from the restaurant and the other people chatting at the table dissipated as I fixated on what David had just shared.

He continued, "Where do you think people go when they die, Emma?" His piercing blue eyes cut through all of my bullshit and walls I thought I had constructed around dealing with this aspect of organ donation.

I took a sip from my margarita.

"Emma, your donor is all around you. When someone dies, they don't just disappear from the universe. They are with us. Let that idea go that you are experiencing all these things and they are not. Let go that you are alone." At that point, I was ugly crying so hard I ran out of napkins to blow my nose. I had known David for about an hour, maybe less, and I felt a connection to him I still can't explain no matter how many times my parents ask me to.

Instead of accepting the things we can't control, I tried to convince David why I didn't deserve to feel this internal peace he was talking about, why I shouldn't let go of the extra weight I carried.

Not even twenty-four hours prior, my session with Dr. J. had ended with a homework assignment for the week to journal about my worthiness outside of my chronic disease and school. She asked me to think about what I deserve without considering other people's emotions or reactions, especially my donor's, and to remember that I am just me: Emma.

It brought me back to the core of where this all started. *Why was I deserving of this extraordinary act of humanity?*

The gift of my heart transplant has placed me on this trajectory that I'm still learning how to graciously receive and include people in along the way. On David's last day, he led a sacred stone ceremony. Previously, I was a skeptic of stones and crystals and their power but that was, of course, before I met David.

Jessica, our host, pulled out her card deck, and David put his brown pouch in the center of the table. He mentioned something about the energy reading the night before amid my emotional breakthrough, but between the talk of my donor, people dying, and letting myself enjoy the rest of the time in Hawai'i, it skipped my mind.

David started the ceremony by reminding us, "Rocks are like people who never go away; rocks are forever." On the table was his bag of crystals that he had been carrying around, and we finally saw what was inside.

One by one, all of us closed our eyes and put our hands in the bag to pull whichever rock spoke to us out. When it was my turn, I felt around the bag, and there were some jagged rough edges and smooth sides, but I had no idea how to figure out "which one spoke to me." So, I stirred all the rocks and went with one that felt flat against my fingers and had curved smooth edges, something to run my fingers along.

Everyone standing in the circle was silent as I looked at my rock. Flipping the rock around in my palm, I decided it looked like a hippo. Once the attention was off me and the next person went, I inspected my rock closely. To my surprise, the crystal I randomly chose wasn't an organic shape or a hippo turned on its side, but an opaque angel.

Everyone's jaw dropped except David's. Instead of commenting on my coincidence, he handed the bag to the next person in our circle. But I still wouldn't give it to him; this rock was just a mere coincidence.

After all six of us picked our rocks, David instructed us to breathe into them. We were preparing our rocks to ground us once we consciously stepped out of the moment we shared together. Rocks are forever, and this rock, my angel, was going to hold onto all this energy forever, no matter the decisions we made when we left. No matter where I lived or what I decided to do in the real, adult world, once I left the farm, this rock collected our spirit and rooted us together. How fitting.

My angel wasn't the only strange coincidence during the ceremony. Jessica laid out her deck of cards, and everyone else shuffled theirs in two nice, neat piles, as you would for a regular deck of cards. But I felt compelled to spread them all out around the table and mix them with my hands in a stirring motion.

Holding my breath, I reached down and randomly chose a card near the center of the mess I had made. It was number sixteen: my lucky number. The front of card sixteen read, "What You Want Wants You," and the back read:

Do you dare to believe that what you want is also wanting you? The genuine desires of your heart are the sacred purpose of the soul, swathed in pleasure. Yet if you have been shamed, judged for, made to feel guilt over, or denied your natural desires or pleasures in any way, you may have developed a very tricky and complicated relationship with the yearnings of your heart. We often learn to distrust our own desires and come to believe that they are something to be overcome or avoided. We may even try to want second best, disbelieving that we are worthy of our first choice, of what we really, genuinely want and would fulfill us deeply. Perhaps we have conditioned ourselves to believe that getting what we want is for others, not us.

This oracle comes with a healing message for you. First, trust in what you truly want—not the substitutions and make-dos, but what would truly bring a sense of passionate, playful purpose and fulfillment to your life. If you genuinely do not know what your heart wants, you will very much enjoy the process of exploring your desires by making gentle and persistent inquiries of yourself. Ask yourself what it is that truly moves you. Give this matter consistent attention without forcing a response.

Your answers may come in a sudden flood, or slowly, over time. As you get to know your genuine desires and give yourself permission to feel and receive them, a powerful sequence is set in motion. Keep dreaming of your fulfillment, but don't imagine it as always awaiting you in some distant future. Instead, play with what it will feel like to be so fulfilled, right now. Give yourself permission to go there. This oracle brings you the message that whether you see it coming or not, your desire is already on its way to you. It's closer than you think and soon you will be able to see it, touch it, feel it, and enjoy it. (*Sacred Rebels Oracle*, Fairchild and Morrison)

As I was reading this aloud to the group, my heart started racing, and I could feel my face heat up. Again, my body physically reacted to the score it kept. (*The Body Keeps the Score*, van der Kolk) The universe had to be screaming at me at this point. In that moment, I started to finally listen.

The angel in my hand was cooling the clamminess of my hands. All along, I was so afraid to ask myself what I desired because what if I didn't get to live long enough to experience it?

Desire is romantic and offers infinite possibilities, but I recognized at twelve years old that infinity is not within reach. Desire is for people who have the answers and have it all figured out; it's for real life, and so far, I had lived in structures that were manufactured by my education, doctor's appointments, and living at home with my parents. There was no time to think about what I desired in that structure; I couldn't imagine then making it this far.

Yet there I was, holding a card that was shouting at me the same things I had tried to ignore and suppress during Dr. J.'s sessions, except it was a random chance encounter with David.

Real life was supposed to be fun and filled with certainty, or at least that is what we are taught in the structures that are built for us. Adults are supposed to know what is going on.

I imagined that when I graduated from college, I would have more of a sense of structure and the transition to jumping right into adult life wouldn't be as harsh as it is. More than anything, I relied on a frivolous daydream about being prepared for whatever what was next was supposed to be because the inverse was, and still is, a huge trigger for me. No one prepared me to have a heart transplant, and I panicked that I was also not prepared to start my life.

Going to Hawai'i was supposed to prolong the period before entering real life, but instead, it jump-started the process because while I was there, I had all the time in the world to pause. The farm that hosted us didn't have a great Wi-Fi connection, forcing us to keep our computers in the closet and be present. We all thought that during the trip we would be proactive and on LinkedIn scouring for job opportunities when we were not working, which in retrospect, was a thoughtful idea.

Even though this trip was just for fun, I told myself that to validate the reason for going and not diving headfirst into a career right away. That said, even being on an island surrounded by my favorite things, I was still anxious as fuck and frustrated that my depression had followed me to this surreal experience. Connecting with David and Jessica and spending so much time outdoors reminded me why I love farming—for not only what it provides but as a practice for healing.

Growing up and working in our home garden with my mom on the weekends to service-learning trips and capstone practicums on farms in Upstate New York, working outside has allowed me to engage all five senses at once, which is one of the most practical ways to ground yourself. Living on the farm on O'ahu, I rekindled and refocused on my relationship with my body without intending to.

Pausing without the distraction of Instagram, the stress of LinkedIn, or watching Netflix most nights granted me the opportunity to re-meet my body and get to know it in a way that I had lost while in college. Instead of hating what I saw in the mirror, I appreciated how much my body had carried me through unconditionally.

At the end of every morning, a massive pile of weeds accumulated on the driveway of all the groundcover we cleared, a trophy of our work that ultimately, we fed to the goats. Holding something tangible that my body had enabled me to do, albeit garden weeds, was part of the structure that led me back to myself.

While it took more time than I thought it would to get out of my head, lean into being present, and shed the idea of what I thought I should be doing post-graduation, there was space and time for me to connect with my spiritual self in ways I thought were spurious before. Connecting with myself by engaging all of my senses forced me to be present and not worry about my future plans or my next heart transplant or what I was going to do when I left Hawai'i.

There is a Hawaiian saying, *"E Malama 'oe I ka 'Āina, e Malama ka 'Āina ia 'oe."* We had the privilege of learning from elders who passed on their stories and explained the meaning: take care of the land, and the land will take care of you. (The Kohala Center, n.d.) Once I understood what it meant and started to believe in it, I found that the saying was another structural bridge that led me back to home: my body. I now know a conducive healing environment for me is mutualistic, one where I can use my body to take care of the land.

I thought of myself as more than a sick human who would die early. I felt strong and capable of making decisions where there is no right or wrong answer, decisions with no directions on how to make them other than listening to myself.

My prayer to repeat three times is, "What I want, wants me, and I am open, willing, and capable to receive it through unconditional love now." (*Sacred Rebels Oracle*, Fairchild and Morrison) Even with part of this sentiment permanently inked on my body, I still need to kindly remind myself that it's okay to desire unconditionally.

This is the same thing Nick has also kindly reminded me since the very beginning of our relationship. "Even if today were your last day, I would still want to be with you because I got to experience what it's like to be with you." I couldn't understand then how he was so sure about what he felt for me. He was so articulate about what he wanted before we started dating without flying across the country and living in the middle of the ocean. I memorized the moment Nick shared that with me and hold it closely because it continues to remind me that I am capable of sharing myself with someone—without having to change any part of me.

Finally allowing myself to believe I am enough, just as I am, without any conditions, is what I wanted from the beginning but was too scared to admit.

Before I left Hawai'i, I wrote myself a postcard: *"Remember sixteen and remind yourself that if you were able to connect with yourself here, you can do it anywhere. You just have to lean in and take the first step and try not to worry about climbing up the others. Find spaces where you can connect with yourself. And do it often because it feels good. It feels like home."*

Now that I am finding my way and working on building my new structure, it's comforting to know where I have been to know where I'm going—north. It fills me with so much gratitude I cry sometimes to be surrounded by people who make exploring this new territory of adulthood easier. David, along with the friends I traveled with and our loving host Jessica, showed me I can connect with myself and how powerful that journey is.

No surgeon, medication, or transplant can take that power away from me. I am actively working on accepting that while my chronic illness is always going to be a part of who I am, this time, I am not letting it make me feel like a lesser person. This time I want to remember that indescribable feeling of connecting with my body and fixate on it, get comfortable with it, and chase it until I truly believe it with my heart and soul.

FIGURING OUT HOW TO LIVE WHILE I'M DYING

I am on the journey of figuring out how to live while I am dying.

Since there doesn't seem to be a textbook answer or clear directions, Dr. J. and I have spent many sessions discussing this question—more specifically, about the balance between the two. I love asking questions. I'm really good at it, so long as I am not the one that has to come up with the answer. Questions are my way of putting the pause into practice.

In fact, the minute I woke up from both my transplant and brain surgery, the first thing I asked was, *Am I okay?* Another pressing question I asked when I woke up from my transplant surgery, after "When can I return to school?" was "Am I going to play soccer and volleyball again?"

Those questions were the first time I processed my intake of the situation.

At the time, I was playing recreational soccer and could have easily collapsed on the field had I not gone to the doctor's office with my dad when I did. I didn't have a preexisting condition, and there weren't health mandates in place that would've ensured all players had preventive cardiac exams. Our team was the Yellow Jackets. I was very concerned about getting back on the field. My nonexistent soccer career seemed the primary motivating factor for my surgery recovery thoughts.

One of the many doctors who came to see me that week during rounds confidently reassured me, "Your transplant should not hold you back from doing anything you want to do. It will enable you to keep living your active life, although I suggest refraining from contact sports, not because you can't physically, it just might hurt getting a ball to the chest more than the average person." I took the joke lightly. I was not into playing football or hockey, so my priorities were still on track. School and soccer were my metrics for getting back to normal.

From my understanding, hearing that right after my transplant surgery led me to believe all of the tubes, wires, beeping machines, chest X-rays, and echocardiograms were behind me. I needed to move again, and the scars on my chest were not going to stop me. I once played in a volleyball tournament the day after I'd had a biopsy procedure.

That motivational speech has kept me moving forward since then.

But now, the questions have gotten more complex. Instead of wondering if I'll be able to play sports again, I am wondering how I can actively live and die simultaneously. Even then, I was afraid if I stayed still, I would lose my momentum and all my progress toward normalcy would go down the drain. Rest was a waste of time when I could be using my heart to enable me to play volleyball and keep up physically with my teammates.

Almost dying is supposed to offer the opportunity to radically change your perspective and meditate three times at a yoga retreat while drinking green juice to get through your midlife crisis. However, almost dying at twelve meant I got ice cream whenever I wanted. My life had yet to really begin, and my commencement of living came at the price of another person's ending.

I convinced myself that I wouldn't be honoring my donor if I lived a values-based life. There was no way it could be fair when my donor probably would not have gotten to graduate from high school or college, discover what they were passionate about, travel to new places, celebrate the new year with loved ones, or have gotten enough warm embraces and kisses from their parents, loved ones, partners, and friends; my list could go on.

I don't know anything about my donor, but I know that I can experience these things because of them. No one ever has enough of these moments. But searching for fairness has not led me to an answer on how to live while we're dying. It has not explained how it's fair that seventeen people, every day, are robbed of moments with their loved ones from the lack of organs and tissues available for transplant. (*Facts and Myths About Organ Donation*, 2022)

With this understanding and awareness, my perspective is heavily nuanced surrounding living.

Now that I have graduated from asking how to maximize my life, most of my therapy sessions are filled with questions of what living a meaningful life looks like in practice with the awareness of how fragile life is. The question for this decade is finding out if there is a possibility for both. Is there room for my journey between living and dying? The "and" or the "in-between" of both extremes hold so much value that I wasn't paying attention until I learned the Greek words Kairos* and Chronos.*

The Greeks' awareness and measurement of time is the key to recalibrating my understanding of living. Authors Yoon and

Barton's research from 2019 about the overreliance on a rigid Chronos sense of time in processes and leadership explains that "Kairos time, is contingent on situations, [that are] socially meaningful and tied to human interactions and opportunities. It is not simply a particular duration in clock time," whereas Chronos time is "measurable, clock- and calendar-based."

Both quantifications of time are meant to complement each other "and should not be seen as two distinguished classifications" because it eliminates the possibility to live in between the "and." The alternative is black and white; I am using my values to make decisions, or I am letting my fear of death to make decisions. I am living, or I am dying.

Reframing my belief about time as opportunities, rather than the minutes, hours, or years I have left, eliminates the internal pressure I put on myself to continuously go above and beyond. I felt like I had to prove myself worthy because I got this extraordinary gift that I never asked for and still can't reason with.

The in-between imploded the ticking time bomb in my chest because it made space for the pause. I can honestly say that embarking on finding my answer has a lot less to do with external accomplishments and more so to do with the amount of Kronos time I have dedicated to my own internal development.

I am starting to redefine what living life to its fullest, while dying, means to me.

THE END IS MY BEGINNING

SO I SHOULD PROBABLY START LIVING

I held my breath in the months leading up to April 1, 2021. The number ten seemed so significant and final, like I wasn't going to experience another anniversary or even another decade.

The looming milestone was with me on my last first day of school, my last fall break, and my last winter break of college. It was especially loud when I finally was able to calm down and manage some stillness.

The shitstorm I put myself through to try to make sense of living with my heart for ten years didn't reveal anything I didn't already know.

The big ten was supposed to bring me all this clarity and closure, like the last chapter of this book. I began this project with the intention that upon completion, the relief from surrendering to all the shit I can't control would finally offer me comfort. Really, my decade anniversary was just another day I got to spend with Nick and my family, drinking good wine.

It has been a little over a decade since the change that radically altered my perspective, and I still don't know what's going on. My clusterfuck of an experience has led me to understand

and appreciate how incredibly fragile life is and how even more delicate living is.

The second chance I received to wake up that morning surrounded by doctors meant that someone else didn't. I'm getting as comfortable as I can with the understanding that my gift means that somewhere, somehow, people had a tremendous loss and there is not a single thing I could've done to change it or stop it from happening. No amount of control or planning could've prepared my life for that giant pivot, and this clarity that I am desperate to discover is probably not going to jump out at me.

By now, I thought I would have all my directions figured out. I would desperately love to relay that I have it all figured out and have surrendered to the idea of living with a chronic illness.

Putting in the work with Dr. J. for over three years was supposed to mean I could ask all the questions I thought I needed and be on my way north. There wouldn't be a reason to pause and reassess or continue working on my interpersonal structural foundation because in my mind, it would be done, and writing this book would tie it all together nicely and neatly.

Wouldn't it be nice if it were that easy? No more needing to put in the work because of the conversations you had in your early twenties when you knew nothing about yourself. To my demise, Dr. J. still doesn't answer my questions and often does something way worse: reassure me that these answers I am looking for might take my lifetime to understand because only then will I be able to tie up all the loose ends.

She reassures me they are called "ends" for a reason, and I am still at the very beginning.

So far, most of my life has been prescribed. Since the very beginning of my life, someone has told me what to do. My

Monday through Friday for the last fifteen years was dictated by a schedule that revolved around classes, assignments, and extracurricular activities.

After my heart transplant, I had to immediately adapt to a new structure that I had no choice to incorporate into my blueprints. Between the meds I take twice a day every day, doctor's appointments and diagnoses, there is little room to go off on a tangent and break the mold. Or at least I am not the person to do that; I thrive in structures that I don't have to create myself because it puts less pressure on me.

In the last year, I have lost most of that structure. It never occurred to me that the transition away from having most of my life structured wouldn't be as liberating as I thought. It's terrifying, and there are so many questions that can't be answered unless I start living. I thought I could address it all right now and be done with it. I thought there was no need to let it carry on into the next year, to torture myself trying to make sense of the last ten-plus years in twelve months and then cross out working through all of my trauma off my to-do list.

Accepting the medical, undeniable fact that my heart is aging, just like the rest of my own organs in my body, seems like giving up. I want to live a long and healthy life but also do things that jeopardize it. I am not perfect, even though I want to be. Openly acknowledging this feels like the thing I am most terrified of: embracing dying.

Unironically, my last semester of college, I took a religion class where every week we discussed fulfillment in our personal lives, community, and ourselves. This class was the first time outside of working with Dr. J. I learned how to analyze my internal data. REL 101 was one of the most impactful experiences I had at Syracuse. You can imagine my debilitating fear when I walked into the chapel for class and two words were projected on the screen in the front of the room in unmissable letters: "Dying Well."

The universe was trying to talk to me, and I didn't want to hear it. Actually, I was doing everything I could to stick my middle finger toward it.

That was the only class I had in-person my entire senior year because of the COVID-19 pandemic, and I thought, *Everyone in the chapel is going to experience my meltdown.* Our professor incorporated pausing often in our classwork to make time for what he called "discernment."

On that specific day, our classwork was writing our own obituary. There have been few times in my life where keeping myself composed was that difficult. I was twelve years old again, and instead of lying on the hospital gurney recovering from my heart transplant, this time, I was imagining what my family would've said at my funeral. What parts of me would I have wanted embraced and carried on from my twelve years of experience on this Earth?

Instead of being uncomfortable, I immediately texted Dr. J. using my notebook as a shield to hide my phone; she had the audacity to tell me to stay present with it. I hoped she meant to send that text to another one of her patients who was not about to face their fear in public. Then to procrastinate even more from doing this activity, I went to the bathroom and cried—a lot.

I was no longer thinking about twelve-year-old me but thirty five-year-old me. Would I get another ten years with this heart? The activity was about one week after my ten-year anniversary, and it all felt too raw. Where were my fucking values of surrendering and acceptance when I needed them? As I was staring at the blank white piece of paper, I didn't want to make a mistake. If I was going to write my own obituary, it had to perfectly outline who I was, especially after surpassing such a big milestone. I wrote:

> "Emma Tyler Rothman was an empath. Some would say that it was her demise, but for Emma, it was her moral compass. Her relationships and connections with her family, friends, and colleagues guided her life. She was operating on borrowed time, and no one would've known unless she told them."

Instead of demanding clarity, which I know makes me feel like shit because it always leads to the worst question, "Why did this happen?" I should've paused. Looking through my course notes later, I never noted my professor talking about fulfilling life as a race to outrun death. In pausing instead of panicking, maybe I could have been able to answer the question our professor had asked us on day one of class: "What do we want most?"

Not even a year ago, I would've said something about a career or saving the world, totally neglecting to mention that I can't do any of that if my health is shit. Now I know that staying healthy is what I want most, and yet here we are: still stuck. I never treated myself like I had a chronic illness, and I never thought of myself like I had a chronic illness.

What I wanted most right after my transplant was probably to go back to middle school, go to college, and when I got to college, be successful and have a job of some sort. It took a lot of trial and error and a lot of hospital visits throughout college to realize all of those things are great, but I can't have any of them if the vessel that holds all my organs isn't properly taken care of.

To remain true to the promise I made you in my author's note about remaining real and unfiltered, I have to admit that I still don't know what I want most. I feel like my answer should be some generic shit about living a values-driven healthy life, but balance doesn't exist.

At least I don't know how to do all of that yet, and I have spent many hours convincing Dr. J. that this expectation is impossible and unfair. My expectation management has never had room for pivots or change, and the difference between now and then is not really what happens moving forward but how I show up.

Inevitably, my heart will get sick again; maybe it will be my kidneys first or another brain surgery, but now I know that whatever happens is my narrative. Right now, what I want most is to hit the pause button and get accustomed to my surroundings.

Since April 1, 2012, I've been sprinting north, and I still don't know where that is. By the time I have some sort of inclination, north changes and my journey pivots.

In the next ten years, instead of expecting myself to overcome all the shit that makes me uncomfortable, I want this book to remind me that pausing doesn't mean stopping or failing to prove I am worthy of this lifesaving gift I received a decade ago. Pausing leaves room for living, and I am starting to accept that in those moments, I am the most alive.

I have to start somewhere.

THE LAST WORD

FROM DR. J.

I can remember the first time I saw a commercial for Prozac on television. I was watching a show with my brother and parents, and as the commercial played, the room fell awkwardly silent and uncomfortable. No one made eye contact. It might as well have been a commercial for tampons or condoms because the discomfort in the room was just as palpable. After the commercial, we continued as if nothing had happened.

Fast forward to today? Thanks especially to social media, we have access now more than ever to topics and conversations around mental health and emotional well-being from everyday people as well as major celebrities. One of my favorite social media memes is a comparison between how older adults whispered to friends or were reluctant even to acknowledge that they were in therapy, while millennials and Gen X, Y, Z, etc. actively share and discuss the content of their therapy sessions with their friends while out to dinner or within their group texts. Trust me, I've seen the screenshots of conversations—both to my amusement and chagrin.

What does this all mean? Well, a few things.

For starters, we are becoming a hell of a lot more comfortable with conversations around mental health, medication, and psychotherapy. It's about damn time that the narrative around mental health is changing. It also means that, in this exploration, we are willing to be more vulnerable. We are more willing to be open to conversations about anxiety, depression, and suicide. We are changing the narrative about and around mental health: less "Oh, just stop being anxious," more "I hear you; I see you. What do you need? How can I support you? Let's figure this out together."

How might this translate into conversations surrounding mental health and transplant for the recipient and donor, as well as their families? Can we have open conversations about the myriad of emotions donors, recipients, and their families feel?

Emma's journey in rewriting her personal narrative jumpstarted when we began working together. It was a tremendous opportunity for her to insert herself into her story instead of watching it from the sidelines.

This heart transplant, while lifesaving, was a situation in which choices were made *for* her. Even though those choices were in her best interest and kept her alive, they also minimized her voice. And to be clear, any parent or guardian would have done the same thing for a young child in massive heart failure.

However, this choice, this "gift of life," also came with heavy responsibility for the rest of her life over which Emma also didn't get a say in. Emma was tasked with carrying the torch of daily medications, frequent routine check-ups, vigilance to bodily sensations, ongoing concerns about rejection, the impact of antirejection and other medications on her entire organ system, how the illness will impact her health, and, more recently, sitting with the thoughts of needing another transplant.

In the transplant world in particular, there is a fine line between, for example, the "what-if" statements that are a hallmark in anxiety disorders and holding space for legitimate concerns such as "What if I go into rejection? What if this cold becomes pneumonia?"

The COVID-19 pandemic took hold of the world and amplified these concerns. In the absence of any longitudinal data about COVID-19 and transplants, Emma had to sit with making decisions about how to live her life in ways that were authentic, meaningful, and kept her as physically healthy as possible.

Many times, there was a substantial disconnect between the advice of her medical team and what she perceived as in her best interest for her emotional well-being.

Our work attempted to bridge that gap and focus less on her final decision and more on a framework for her to make decisions. While we couldn't be sure of the outcome, Emma could find some peace and clarity in how she made decisions for herself and took back some authority and agency in her daily life.

How did we do this? Initially, by just creating the space to do so: holding space. How do we exactly create and hold space, though? To start, we can simply sit with the notion that there is room for more. We can acknowledge and validate the messiness of having conflicting emotions. We utilized mindfulness-related strategies to notice and explore what would come up in Emma as we sat with these (and many other) questions. Allowing space to pause, to breathe.

We often sat with the theme of "being grateful" during sessions. Emma was told numerous times how "grateful" she should feel to be alive, and even said herself as she struggled with the notion that this "gift of life" meant that not only did someone else die, but they or their families chose to give another person (or often, persons), the very opportunity to do what that family would be grieving the loss of—their loved one's existence.

Was there space to feel *anything* else? Initially, Emma didn't think so. What would it mean to others, especially her donor family, if she was anything *but* grateful? What about when the daily responsibilities and burden stemming from this "gift of life" was, some days, seemingly unbearable?

Can you imagine a time in which someone told you how you should feel about something? Losing a job, going through a breakup, experiencing the death of a loved one? Someone might have told you that you were "so much better off without that job or person," or, in the case of death, that your loved one was "in a better place."

And yes, they might be right, in a practical and logical way, but does that help your grieving heart at that moment? Probably not. And not only is it not helpful, but it might also feel invalidating because the message you are hearing is about how you *should* feel and doesn't hold space for how you *are* feeling.

Eventually, the opinions of others start to carry more weight than honoring our own voice and feelings. We don't want to rock the boat and assert ourselves or challenge others' ways of thinking. We do this by quietly agreeing, the good old-fashioned "smile and nod," silencing our own voice in the service of minimizing or avoiding someone else's discomfort. This often leads to guilt and shame for feeling something, anything, different from what you have been told you should feel.

The unintended consequence of this is that over time, we end up mindfucking ourselves into believing that our thoughts and feelings don't hold as much weight as those of others around us. In turn, the ability to trust ourselves wavers, and seeking the opinions of others on how we should think, feel, and make decisions becomes the norm.

As a result, the story changes. The narrative becomes something other than what we intended it to be. If we let it go on long enough, we may find ourselves telling a story and living a life that feels unfamiliar and inauthentic. We become disconnected from our values and how we want to live in service of attempting to minimize the noise of feedback from those around us. For Emma, giving herself permission to have an opinion, a voice, a feeling, or a thought that may run contrary to those of her closest family and friends was an incredibly intense process for her and, in many ways, the impetus for this book.

For Emma, this is where creating and holding space began.

For patients living with chronic illness or pain, I often see them scrupulously document their health histories in a way that the best physician can't. This level of detail serves a few interests; it helps them remember what was said in the appointment, for example.

However, it also helps the patient feel like they have some control over a process in which they feel very powerless or helpless to change—pages and pages of moment-to-moment details of appointments, medications, and symptoms. Perhaps, by controlling their medical narrative, they can control their symptoms, their outcomes, their physical and emotional pain, and their suffering.

Now, I'm not saying that's not necessary, and I would *never* tell a patient not to do that, especially if their doctor was asking them to, which none were—not to that degree, anyway.

Instead, I ask "What's the cost of doing this? What are you giving up or taking on by doing this?" We would then begin a conversation about values—the direction they want their lives to take—and what those goals might look like.

This requires patients to disarm themselves. It requires them to let go of how they identify with their illness—its impact on their past and their fears about the future—and shift focus on how they want to live their life *now*.

In essence, it requires surrender.

Most people have two reactions when they hear or read the word *surrender*; they either exhale or tense up further. Maybe the thought of surrender means letting go of what isn't serving you anymore, and that relieves, exhilarates, or scares the shit out of you—or all of that combined. Either way, it means becoming vulnerable. In fact, the act of mindfully, peacefully, and purposefully accepting and surrendering can be one of the biggest acts of self-love.

In one of our more recent sessions, Emma noted that "surrendering felt like dying." So much of health-related terminology revolves around "fighting for your life" or "fighting through treatment," and here I was, inviting Emma to...not do that, to stop fighting, to just *be*.

The theme of resistance as the inverse of surrender is a constant undercurrent in psychotherapy, and Emma's process was no different. However, some of Emma's most difficult yet transformative moments in session are when she lets go of control and allows vulnerability to start to seep in to expand her emotional repertoire and let go of the guilt and shame for feeling anything but "grateful."

Fear, sadness, anger: they were all invited in, and Emma learned to just notice whatever emotion comes up in that moment without feeling the need to *do* anything with it, without the need to justify it. This lesson is a daily one, and the teacher—life—will always show up to teach it.

So much of this book and the act of Emma rewriting her transplant narrative was paying attention to and honoring the raw thoughts and emotions that came up as she explored the past ten years. It was riddled with unexpected emotional detours—the depths of which she was not initially prepared for. And, in some ways, neither was I.

Despite my years of experience working in medical rehabilitation settings with brain injury patients, Emma was my first transplant patient. It was a great opportunity to model vulnerability in sessions. That ranged from "Emma, I don't know much about this; can you help me understand?" to "Emma, I have not a fucking clue," delivered and received with a lot of laughter and snark. Needless to say, Emma certainly learned, and I was reminded that vulnerability doesn't always have to feel dark and heavy.

Through Emma connecting to her values and exploring the direction she wants her life to move in and acknowledging her emotions and committing to putting one foot in front of the other, you as the reader get to bear witness to a truly extraordinary young woman's journey into one of the most important things we can learn to do: trust ourselves.

To trust ourselves is to be our own lighthouse in the storm, to trust ourselves to make values-based decisions about situations or people, no matter how rocky the seas. Of note, this doesn't mean there is not room for others to support us. Rather, it encourages us to prioritize the relationship we are guaranteed to have for the rest of our lives—the one with ourselves.

Trust is not loud or boastful; rather, it is calm, consistent, and steadfast. The healthiest relationships with ourselves and others often reveal trust as their backbone. In our initial sessions, it was critical to not only lay the groundwork for Emma to feel safe to explore whatever came up, but for her to understand the ways in which I would support her through the process. With these clear boundaries in place, the therapeutic relationship has grown on *her* terms.

As a result, she began to trust herself to steer her ship wherever she wanted to and explore the uncharted areas of her mind and heart that were previously off-limits to her, *by* her. The initial trust in me, the process, and most importantly, with herself, made space for her to surrender a way of living that wasn't working anymore.

Surrendering is messy, painful, exhilarating, and freeing. It is *not* a one-time transaction.

It is a daily exercise in deciding *how you want to show up in life*—when to push, when to pull back.

This book as a reflection of Emma's walk through the last ten years as a transplant recipient not only graciously invites us in and gives an intimate view of the transplant world, but it is an exercise in Emma rewriting her narrative of her health and her heart, both physically and emotionally speaking. The lesson learned? Control is, in fact, surrender.

Thank you, Emma, for allowing all of us to bear witness to your journey and to the surrender.

MY THANK-YOU NOTES

I used to dread writing thank-you notes until I understood how much easier it is to share compassion and appreciation for others than it is to receive it for yourself. Since we were kids, my mom enforced the habit of writing thank-you notes, and I used to hate taking the time to pause and write. Now, fifteen years later, I am so grateful she laid the foundation for practicing gratitude.

However, I've never written a book before, so here it goes.

My beloved donor: We're in this together—for the long run.

Mom and Dad: You both are part of my heart and soul. There will never be enough texts or notes to convey how incredibly grateful I am for the unconditional lengths both of you go to, to support me in all aspects of my life, not just the medical parts. I love you.

Keri: Thank you for being my big sister when I know it's not always easy or fun. My kitchen table is wherever the last laugh is with you.

Grandma: Our phone calls brought me back to this on days when I didn't think I could write a single word. This book is a product of sharing the unconditional love you send me with everyone who reads this. You told me to write a book, and we finally did it. *Shabbat Shalom* and *Ani Ohevet Otach* for today, tomorrow, and forever.

Nick Tyler: When I wanted to *bleep bloop blop* and give up, every time you brought me back to Earth. I love the shit out of you.

Everyone at NDP and the Creators Institute: Thank you for giving a very depressed and anxious storyteller the space to process authentically. Telling the truth isn't easy, and it would've been so much harder without your support.

Michelle: Thank you for being a badass and fearlessly reminding me why I started this project in the first place. I wouldn't have crossed the finish line without you.

David: During our last meeting when I asked you for any words of wisdom and you responded, "I don't know, no one really fucking knows anything," I knew our time together was meant to be. Thank you for your bluntness and for making a really fucking difficult time a little funny.

To The Morgan Stanley Children's Hospital Congenital Heart Center Program for Pediatric Cardiomyopathy, Heart Failure, and Transplantation — Dr. Chen, Dr. A., Dr. Rocky, Dr. Richmond, Dr. Zuckerman, Lisa, Eunice, Meredith, Hannah, Amy, Ali, Marilyn, and the cath lab team, all the PICU nurses, as well as Dr. O'Connor, Dr. Josh and his team at the Beth, and all the other medical heroes in that building who dedicate their time to treating really sick kids: Even though I am learning to make a new home down the street and around the corner, my heart will always belong to you all. Thank you for saving a really sick kid's life.

Dr. J.: Don't let this get to your head, but this book wouldn't be complete without you.

David and Jessica: I once heard that only the impossible ever happens. So thank you, Jessica, for letting us into your home, and thank you both for letting me into your hearts. *Mahalo.*

Dean Konkol: Thank you for the discernments we had in your office—they continue to profoundly impact my life. This book is proof.

Dr. Harris and her spring semester Gender and Disability class: Thank you for your genuine curiosity about this project. And Dr. Harris, thank you for introducing me to the world of binaries and disability and pop culture. If it weren't for your class, it would've taken me a hell of a lot longer to realize and accept that I am chronically ill.

Evan: Thank you for making Syracuse feel like home. Your memory will forever be a blessing.

Gill: Thanks for being my silly little friend and reminding me that my chaos is beautiful enough to be on the front cover of a book. Your energy makes all of my days brighter.

To the Hearts for Emma past and current crew, including all the volunteers who help facilitate our ideas to fruition: There's no us without you.

To all my campaign supporters and beta readers*: Thank you for joining this journey before there was a clear destination.

Alyssa D'Addio	Barbara Robbins
Amy E. Robinson	Bobbi Anderson
Ana Ximenes	Brian Konkol*
Anastasia Breeze	Bruce Harris
Andrew Dipkin	Caitlin Sanders
Andrew J. Seymour	Carolyn Smaka
Annie Conley	Christine Maccallum
Audrey Miller	Clara Nunziato
Avital Abraham	Dana Shectman

Daniel Harris
Daniel Rothman
Daniela Linkewer-Schwab
Danielle Barba
David DeBole*
David Fox
Dawn Nicholas
Derek Wallace
Diane Seymour
Eileen Heider
Eilidh Brady
Elisse Glennon
Eliza Lunt
Elizabeth Atkins
Elizabeth Stamler
Ellen Berman
Ellen Levenberg
Emily Serna
Eric Koester
Erin Swisher
Eunice Clark
Eve Minson
Genevieve Williamson
Georgeann Vignari
Gillian Farrugia
Grandma Annette
Hannah Isaacs-Arkin
Higgins Marilyn
Imran Nuri
Isabella Maloney
Jackson Rosenblatt
Jacob deHahn

Jacquelyn Plick
Jamie Waxman
Jane Dausch
Jane Maloney
Janet Perino
Jason Kuperberg
Jean Schroder
Jen Wilkins
Jenna M. Walmer
Jennifer Tam
Joan Singer
Jodi Most
Joel and Michelle Abraham
John Vignari
Joy Rothman
Judy Epstein
Julia Howard-Flanders
Kaitlin McGovern
Karyn Vitagliano
Kate Christie
Katherine Mackenzie
Kathryn Comer
Kathy and Dan Ruscitto
Katie Romanovich
Kayla Simon
Kelly Bertog
Kelly Drake
Kelsey Hart
Keri Rothman*
Kimberly Capece
Kirsten Hotchkiss
Larry Rothman

Lauren Carosi
Lauren Marks-Cabanas
Lauren Plattman
Laurie O'Connell-Klein
Leisa Judah
Linda Dickerson
Linda Jastrzebski
Linda Nieporent
Lisa DiNardo
Lisa G. Black
Lori Klein
Maggie Feeney
Margaret R. Post
Marge Cohen
Marilyn Dipkin
Marisa Spitz
Mark and Nancie Rothman
Marne Brown
Mary Kiernan
Matthew Barba
Matthew Kylander
Meisha Rainman
Melissa Gagliardi
Michael Ennis
Michael Penziner
Michelle Miller
Natalie Darwin
Nick Barba
Noelle Gotthhardt
Olivia Babu
Owen Clyne
Paige Phillips

Patrick Linehan
Patti Baldowski
Patti DiSanto*
Phoebe Darwin
Phoebe Hicks
Rhiannon Ramirez
Robin Lyons
Ronnie Moskowitz
Rosemarie Del Grosso
Sally Isaacs
Sam Hollander
Sandra Nussenfeld
Sarah Cassidy
Sarah Vollenbroek
Scott Bartsch
Scott Catucci
Scott Issen
Seth Reed
Shannon Lipari
Stephanie Walker
Steve Rothman
Susan Barba
Susan Sedwin
Tammy J. Ryan*
Tina Hrabak
Tolga O.
Trevor J. Aschmies
Wendy Sciara
Will DeVito

A special thank you to my beta readers, whose continued support carried me to the finish line. Your feedback was vital in making this book something worth reading. My hope is that you all give yourself the same grace and compassion you shared with me throughout this process.

With all the love and gratitude in the universe,
Emma

GLOSSARY

One of the first things I'm asked when people find out I had a heart transplant is if I know who my donor is or if I have met their family. I try to understand where they are coming from and remember that even though all of this is familiar to me, it's not to most people. I try to not take it personally when they casually ask these intrusive questions.

With this in mind, I wanted to take a moment and briefly explain the major components and aftercare of heart transplants from the perspective of a patient, not a clinician. It's extraordinary how hard our bodies work without us having to program them to do this. Over the last ten years, I have been asked many questions—and asked questions myself—about what all this means.

Sometimes I forget I don't have a doctoral degree in cardiology and get frustrated I don't know the answers, or when I do have the wherewithal to ask, the answer is not what I wanted to hear. A clinician's perspective and analysis are profusely different from a patient's, and my hope is to explain what I can in an accessible way. While every patient's journey to and from transplant is different, there are similar terms and processes for all of us defined below.

HELPFUL TRANSPLANT AND OTHER TERMS DEFINED (MOSTLY) BY A CARDIAC PATIENT

Cardiac Arrest

- This happens when your heart suddenly stops beating. My heart was arresting so much that I needed a medically induced coma.

Cardiac biopsy/heart catheter

- Biopsies are procedures that give clinical teams more specific insight on the health of your heart. During the biopsy, a long wire (catheter) travels through a blood vessel in your neck or groin and takes pictures, as well as a microscopic piece of the tissue surrounding the heart. Doctors assess the microscopic tissue under a microscope and use the data collected from the biopsy to ensure that your body is not rejecting the new heart.

Cardiologist

- A cardiologist is a doctor that specializes in heart function and diseases of the heart. My cardiologist team became my primary care physician (PCP) posttransplant.

Catheterization Lab (cath lab)

- A small surgical suite where biopsies are performed.

Clinic (for heart transplant recipients)

- Clinic is where outpatient doctor's appointments are held for patients recovering or waiting for a transplant. The further out from transplant a recipient gets, the less often they must go for check-ups. After my transplant, I went back to the hospital twice a week for a noninvasive

visit for a couple of months. Gradually, it went down
to once a week, then every other week, and so on. Ten
years posttransplant, I aim to schedule an appointment
every six months, which I would never have imagined
when I was sitting in the lab room twice a week with
bruises lining my arms. As I am transitioning out of
pediatric care and into adult cardiology care, I am learning that the tests that were part of my routine as a kid
are not the standard metric anymore.

- During clinic visits, my team comprised of heart failure
  physicians, nurse practitioners, phlebotomists, cardio-
  vascular technicians, child life specialists, and nurses.
  Noninvasive and invasive visits are the two main types of
  check-ups. During invasive visits, I have an EKG, echo, lab
  work, a clinic visit where I see my doctors, and a biopsy.
  During noninvasive visits, there is no biopsy scheduled.

CAT Scan

- An imaging test that is more detailed than an X-ray.
  "The scan combines a series of X-rays taken from different angles around your body and uses a computer
  processor to create cross-sectional images of the bones,
  blood vessels, and soft tissues inside your body." (MAYO
  CLINIC, 2022) I got a CAT scan of my brain.

Child Life Specialist

- Child Life Specialists are health care professionals
  who usually are the only ones in the room not worried
  about your physical state but more concerned with your
  mental state. They provide support to children and their
  loved ones to navigate the chaos of being in the hospital.

I am forever grateful for the child life team where I had my transplant. They supported me in ways I didn't know I needed at the time and always had an endless supply of DVDs, crafts, and funny stories.

Chronos Time

- The Greek word for time that is measurable by clocks and calendars. For example, attending class from 12:45 p.m.–2:00 p.m. is Chronos time.

Coding

- A generic term for hospital emergencies: In my case, my heart coded. This means my heart stopped. Each hospital is different, but in general, it means that a patient is in cardiac arrest and needs resuscitation or "the code team."

Cognitive Behavioral Therapy (CBT)

- The best way I can explain CBT is rewiring your brain to replace behaviors or thought patterns that are distorted, self-judgmental, or anxiety-driven with new ones that serve you. This is the kind of therapy I am practicing with Dr. J. I have learned the skill of recognizing my tendencies that are not rooted in my values but in my all-consuming emotions. CBT takes time, which is the real kicker for high-functioning anxiety-driven people (like me). It took over four years to finally feel confident enough in my skill set to start applying what I learn in session to my day-to-day.

Congenital Heart Disease (CHD)

- Heart diseases or complications that are been present since birth.

Deceased Donor

- Deceased donors are donors that are no longer living. Heart transplants are from a deceased donor.

- There is a common myth that people who register as organ donors don't receive critical care should they be in a life-threatening situation because clinicians know they are registered and therefore let them die because they want to harvest their organs.

- That is ridiculous. Everyone, no matter if they are registered to be an organ donor or not, receives the exact same appropriate treatment in life-threatening situations. Nurses are not spending time looking up your registration history; rather, they are focused on doing their job—keeping you alive. "Specially trained medical practitioners from the OPO go to the hospital to see if the patient is medically suitable for organ donation *after* the patient is declared brain dead." Patients can only donate organs if they are medically cleared and have consent from the state or national registry or their loved ones. (UNOS, n.d.)

Dermatologist

- Doctors and medical professionals who specialize in treating and taking care of the skin.

Discharge

- The moment of freedom: leaving the hospital and going back home.

Donor Family

- Loved ones of a deceased donor, usually family members.

- Reaching out to donors is an extremely personal and vulnerable decision. Usually, recipients have to wait six months before reaching out to their donor and can't do it themselves. We communicate through the hospital where we had our surgery or the OPO for that hospital's region.

Donor Matching

- Donor matching is based specifically on "medical and biological factors and is automated through the United Network for Organ Sharing's (UNOS) computer matching system." (UNOS, n.d.) The recipient will be matched with a donor based on many factors (e.g., blood type, age, health status), but social factors like income status, race, and religion are not taken into consideration in accordance with UNOS matching criteria that were written by recipients, doctors, and the Organ Procurement and Transplantation Network (OPTN) Board of Directors.

Donor Registration List

- The donor registry list is a national database where patients with organ failure are listed once their clinical team determines they need to receive a transplant. The nonprofit United Network for Organ Sharing (UNOS) is the Organ Procurement and Transplantation Network (OPTN) for the United States that manages the national transplant waiting list. (UNOS, n.d.)

Echocardiogram (Echo)

- An echocardiogram is another common test that is an ultrasound of your heart. The ultrasound produces pictures and measurements to make sure that your ventricles and atrium are the right size, are not blocked, and are pumping blood properly, among many other things. This takes about a half hour; I like to make myself a playlist beforehand and listen to it to make the test go by faster.

Electrocardiography (EKG)

- Every day after my transplant and at every check-up, I have an EKG done. EKGs are the least intrusive and least painful medical test during clinic visits. A technician places stickers all over your chest, legs, and arms and connects leads to the stickers. After about a couple of seconds, the computer beeps, and the test is over. Setting up is the longest part of the exam.

- These tests ensure that my heart is pumping blood properly and that my heartbeats were at a normal rate days after my new heart was still getting acquainted with its new home.

Genetic Testing

- Since no one in my family had heart disease (that we knew of), my family and I wanted to ensure that none of my other family members were predisposed to cardiomyopathy. A specialist collected a saliva sample from me and my parents, hoping to better understand our genetic history or detect any possible mutations.

Gynecologist

- Doctors and medical professionals who specialize in treating reproductive and sexual health.

Hypertrophic Cardiomyopathy

- Hypertrophic cardiomyopathy is the swelling of the muscle around the heart. When I was twelve, cardiomyopathy was explained to me using a soccer ball. My heart was the size of a soccer ball when it should have been roughly the size of my fist. Because of the enlarged muscle, my heart had to work harder to do all of its jobs.

Immune System

- The immune system protects the body from outside germs that cause sickness.

Induced coma/Intubation

- Before I had my heart transplant, I was so unstable that I was medically put in a coma, meaning a machine was breathing for me via a plastic tube down my throat that was keeping my airway open (intubation).

Internalized Ableism

- "Internalized ableism is when a person consciously or unconsciously believes in the harmful messages they hear about disability and applies them to themselves." (Medical News Today, Zawn) For example, believing that you, a disabled person, are a burden to society or are needy for asking or needing accommodations (like a ramp or larger menu font size) in public space. Yet, these spaces were designed without you or your needs in mind.

Kairos Time

- The Greek word for time measured as opportunities or meaningful experiences. Instead of thinking about passing the hour and fifteen minutes of class time, reframing the thought to opportunities to learn becomes a flexible experience. Learning is no longer a fixed measurable outcome, but a fluid experience that is impacted by your environment, not just the numbers on the clock.

Lab Work

- Lab work is vital to maintaining the health of a transplant. Clinical teams analyze blood work to get an inside look at how the body is doing. For example, blood work can determine how the body is handling medications, if the body is sick or about to get sick, or if a deficiency in a vitamin or mineral could be contributing to symptoms. Labs are timed and drawn before antirejection medication is taken in the morning to get a more accurate read of how the body is handling all the chaos.

Living Donor

- Living donors can donate part of or their whole organ while they are still alive. Kidneys and livers are the most common types of living donor transplants because family members, friends, or strangers can donate their organs if they biologically match the recipient's needs.

Meds

- Most recipients take antirejection medication (meds) to suppress the body's immune response to minimize the opportunity for it to reject the donated organ. I will be taking antirejection meds for the rest of my life: twelve hours apart every day, along with a handful of other brightly colored pills.

Moyamoya Disease (MMD)

- Moyamoya disease (MMD) is "a blood vessel disorder in which the carotid artery in the skull becomes blocked or narrowed, reducing blood flow to your brain" (Mayo Clinic Staff, 2022). This one is hard to explain without medical terms; one of the highway systems that is responsible for carrying blood to my brain was blocked. Instead of normal traffic flow, my brain found other routes to carry the same volume but on much smaller roads (arteries) that are not built to handle that amount of traffic.

- I found it interesting to note that MMD is the most common pediatric cerebrovascular disease in East Asian regions. Yes, East Asian regions, not North American or even European regions. (Progress in Moyamoya Disease, Shang, S., Zhou, D., Ya, J. Li, S., Yang, Q., Ding, Y., Ji, X., Meng, R.)

Nephrologist

- Doctors and medical professionals who specialize in treating and taking care of the kidneys.

Neurologist

- Doctors and medical professionals who specialize in treating and taking care of the brain.

Organ Procurement Organization (OPO)

- Every transplant hospital program works with an OPO, although not every hospital has a cardiac transplant program. Mine was in New York City. "OPOs are not-for-profit organizations responsible for recovering organs from deceased donors for transplantation in the United

States. There are fifty-seven OPOs, each mandated by federal law to perform this lifesaving mission in their assigned donation service area. They work with a decedent's family during the emotional discussion about potential donation in order to facilitate the organ procurement and transplantation process." (UNOS, n.d.) The OPO for New Jersey is the New Jersey Sharing Network.

Organ Rejection

- The body can confuse the new organ, tissue, or cornea as a foreign threat and start to attack it. The immune system's job is to keep the body healthy by eliminating any foreign germs, and the body doesn't know that the specific transplanted organ is supposed to be there. The antirejection medication weakens the immune system so there is less of a chance of it rejecting the new organ.

Pediatric Cardiac Intensive Care Unit (PICU)

- The PICU is the most critical care inpatient floor at the hospital. When I was first admitted to the hospital, I was sent right to the PICU and stayed there before and after my transplant. In the PICU, patients are watched vigilantly and are often hooked up to machines and take meds that can only be distributed in that kind of care setting.

Suppressed Immune System

- For heart transplants to stay healthy, the immune system needs to be suppressed (weakened) so it doesn't attack the new heart. I will be immunocompromised for the rest of my life—meaning that my body is more susceptible to illnesses because I don't have as strong of a defense system to filter out bacteria, viruses, or other toxins.

- This means that if I do get sick, it takes longer to leave my system and in extreme cases, could potentially turn into something fatal. I remember explaining to professors that a common cold isn't something I can always work through. In the past, it has taken me months to feel completely normal after contracting the sniffles or a common virus.

- Most of the time, sleep is the best and only remedy, but in environments that promote burnout (e.g., going to college or being a twenty-something) taking the time to listen to my body or explain to outsiders that I need to take time because of a cold can feel invalidating.

The New Jersey Sharing Network
- The New Jersey Sharing Network (NJSN) is the OPO for the state of New Jersey. They work "to recover and place donated organs and tissue, support donor families, honor the legacy of those who gave the gift of life, and raise awareness about the power of organ donation and transplantation." (NJ Sharing Network, n.d.)

Triage Room
- A small hospital room where a patient's vital signs (temperature, blood pressure, oxygen levels of the blood and heart rate) are taken and their medical condition and stability are assessed.

504 School Plan
- "Plans designed to help parents of students with physical or mental impairments in public schools, or publicly funded private schools, work with educators to design

customized educational plans. These 504 plans legally ensure that students will be treated fairly at school." (Education Plans, Bachrach)

- For example, my 504 plan included attendance accommodations because when I was in high school, I missed class for hospital visits and because I was sick so often.

For more information about all things concerning organ and tissue donation and transplantation and the Organ Procurement and Transplantation Network, visit www.unos.org.

APPENDIX

A NOTE FROM EMMA

American Transplant Foundation. "Facts and Myths about Transplant." *Facts and Myths*. February 3, 2022.
https://www.americantransplantfoundation.org/about-transplant/facts-and-myths/.

Health Resources and Services Administration. "Organ Donor Statistics."
Learn About Donation, March 2022.
https://www.organdonor.gov/learn/organ-donation-statistics.

"National OPTN Data (All Donors)." OPTN metrics. Accessed June 16, 2022.
https://insights.unos.org/OPTN-metrics/#shiny-tab-tx_details.

"US on Pace to Top 40,000 Transplants in a Single Year for First Time." UNOS,
August 5, 2021.
https://unos.org/news/on-pace-for-40000-transplants-record/.

WHAT IS A CHRONIC DISEASE? WHO DECIDES?

Bachrach, Steven J. "504 Education Plans." Newmours KidsHealth.
The Nemours Foundation, September 6, 2016.
https://kidshealth.org/en/parents/504-plans.html.

Taussig, Rebekah. *Sitting Pretty: The View from My Ordinary Resilient Disabled Body*. New York: HarperOne, 2020.

Villines, Zawn. "What Is Ableism, and What Is Its Impact?" Edited by Debra
Sullivan. *Medical News Today*. Medical News Today, November 7, 2021.
https://www.medicalnewstoday.com/articles/ableism.

I HATE THE WORD SHOULD

Bowler, Kate. *No Cure for Being Human (and Other Truths I Need to Hear)*. New
York: Random House, 2021.

van der Kolk, Bessel A. *The Body Keeps the Score: Brain, Mind, and Body in the Healing of Trauma*. New York: Viking Penguin, 2014.

NOT EVERYTHING HAPPENS FOR A REASON
Brown, Brené. "The Power of Vulnerability." Filmed March 2012 in Long Beach, CA. TED video, 17:52. https://www.ted.com/talks/brene_brown_the_power_of_vulnerability?language=en.

Brown, Keah. *The Pretty One: On Life, Pop Culture, Disability, and Other Reasons to Fall in Love with Me*. New York: Atria Paperback, 2019.

Donate Life NJ. *New Jersey Hero Act Summary*. Accessed June 28, 2022. https://www.nj.gov/oag/hts/downloads/NJ_Hero_Act.pdf.

WHAT IS ENOUGH?
Bowler, Kate. *No Cure for Being Human: (and Other Truths I Need to Hear)*. New York: Random House, 2021.

Brown, Keah. *The Pretty One: On Life, Pop Culture, Disability, and Other Reasons to Fall in Love with Me*. New York: Atria Paperback, 2019.

THE THING ABOUT EXCEPTING THE LOVE YOU THINK YOU DESERVE
van der Kolk, Bessel A. *The Body Keeps the Score: Brain, Mind, and Body in the Healing of Trauma*. New York: Viking Penguin, 2014.

Brown, Keah. *The Pretty One: On Life, Pop Culture, Disability, and Other Reasons to Fall in Love with Me*. New York: Atria Paperback, 2019.

WHAT I WANT, WANTS ME
Fairchild, Alana, and Skye Morrison. *Sacred Rebels Oracle: Guidance for Living a Unique and Authentic Life*. Woodbury: Llewellyn Worldwide, LTD., 2015.

van der Kolk, Bessel A. *The Body Keeps the Score: Brain, Mind, and Body in the Healing of Trauma*. New York: Viking Penguin, 2014.

"Kū ʻĀina Pā: Guiding Principles." The Kohala Center. Accessed June 28, 2022. https://kohalacenter.org/kuainapa/ku-aina-pa-guiding-principles.

FIGURING OUT HOW TO LIVE WHILE I'M DYING
American Transplant Foundation. "Facts and Myths about Transplant." *Facts and Myths*. February 3, 2022. https://www.americantransplantfoundation.org/about-transplant/facts-and-myths/.

Yoon, I. H., and Barton, A. "Turnaround Leaders' Shifting Gears in Chronos and Kairos Time," *Journal of Educational Administration* 57, no. 6 (2019): 690–707. https://doi-org.libezproxy2.syr.edu/10.1108/JEA-08-2018-0139.

GLOSSARY

Mayo Clinic. "CT Scan." Mayo Clinic Tests and Procedures. Mayo Foundation for Medical Education and Research, January 6, 2022. https://www.mayoclinic.org/tests-procedures/ct-scan/about/pac-20393675.

Mayo Clinic Staff. "Moyamoya Disease." Diseases and Conditions. Mayo Foundation for Medical Education and Research, May 1, 2021. https://www.mayoclinic.org/diseases-conditions/moyamoya-disease/symptoms-causes/syc-20355586.

Shang, S., Zhou, D., Ya, J. Li, S., Yang, Q., Ding, Y., Ji, X., Meng, R. "Progress in Moyamoya Disease." *Neurosurgical Review* 43, no. 2 (June 18, 2018): 371–82. https://doi.org/10.1007/s10143-018-0994-5.

UNOS. "Deceased Organ Donation Process." Accessed June 29, 2022. https://unos.org/transplant/deceased-donation/.

UNOS. "How We Match Organs." UNOS. Accessed June 29, 2022. https://unos.org/transplant/how-we-match-organs/.

UNOS. "Organ Procurement Organizations: Increasing Organ Donation." Organ Procurement Organizations. Accessed June 29, 2022. https://unos.org/transplant/opos-increasing-organ-donation/.

UNOS. "United Network for Organ Sharing FAQs." UNOS. Accessed June 28, 2022. https://unos.org/about/faqs/.

"What We Do: NJ Sharing Network." NJ Sharing Network. NJ Sharing Network. Accessed June 30, 2022. https://www.njsharingnetwork.org/what-we-do/.

www.ingramcontent.com/pod-product-compliance
Lightning Source LLC
Chambersburg PA
CBHW052008150726
47999CB00004B/1573